LISTEN UP The Lives of Quincy Jones

Based on the Warner Bros. motion picture LISTEN UP The Lives of Quincy Jones

Warner Books
666 Fifth Avenue, New York, N.Y. 10103
Printed in the United States of America
First Printing November 1990
10 9 8 7 6 5 4 3 2 1
ISBN: 0-446-39233-2 (cassette pkg.)
ISBN: 0-446-39286-3 (CD pkg.)

LISTEN UP The Lives of Quincy Jones

Dedicated to those

who have the courage

to realize their visions,

who overcome the obstacles

and turn back to light

the way for others.

Conceived and Edited by
Courtney Sale Ross

Co-Created and Designed by
Frankfurt Gips Balkind

Essay by
Nelson George

WARNER BOOKS
A Time Warner Company

Project Director
Kent Alterman
Editorial Director
Danny Abelson
Design Director
Kent Hunter
Designers
Thomas Bricker
Riki Sethiadi
Johan Vipper
Contributing Editor
Lee Jeske
Essay Edited by
Wendy Wolf
Photo Researcher
Cindy Joyce
Print Production Director
Bonnie Goldberg
Production Coordinators
Julie Glantz
Stacey Spencer
Production
Shirley C. Beyer
Harold Hall
George Matthaei
James Rabkin
Robert Salazar
Carlos E. Serrano
Electronic Page Layout
Jamie Barnett
Paul Delsignore
Bradford Lowry
Robert Rainey
Jeffrey Sherman
Jeff Zoda
Printing by
Heritage Press

Special Thanks to
Lori Schiaffino
Lloyd Jones
Jolie Jones Levine
Jerold Kayden
Melle Mel
Kimiko Jackson
Stacy Turner
and all the people at
Quincy Jones Productions
and Cort Productions

This is for Nicole.

Sometimes I wish I had a steady job. —Quincy

early years

Lloyd and I were in bed together one night...

we had slept a little bit...

and the thunder woke us up,

the lightning...

WHANG!

It just **crashed** through the window...

and the rain just came pouring down right after the thunder

and the lightning, and we were **terrified.**

It just came pouring down...the shade started to make noise

against the window...We realized that we were home alone...

and **we freaked.**

Nobody was there, you know,

there was nobody there.

–Quincy

9

That's the last time I saw her, until I was 15. And

When Mrs. Jones became ill,

so, emotionally, you say, "Well, I can't depend on a

they had to take her to the mental hospital.

mother, because

And Quincy and Lloyd

QUINCY AND LLOYD, 1935

I don't have one.

So I don't need

one!" I guess

wanted to know, "Why, Lucy?"

trauma gets frozen at the peak. I'm sure that affected

I had no answers. —Lucy Jackson, neighbor

my relationship with women later. –Quincy

INTRODUCTION

In the summer of 1982, Quincy Jones sat behind the control board in a dimly lit room off the recording area at Westlake Studios in Los Angeles. He was putting the finishing touches on a Donna Summer cut and needed a tambourine track for the final mix. It was a minor piece in a major production, but the young percussionist seemed terribly nervous. Quincy quickly picked up on the fact that she felt intimidated and set out to put her at ease. He walked her around the studio, his arm slung casually around her neck as he whispered a few jokes to break the tension. When she seemed ready to record, he left her alone in the studio and went back to the controls, and she began to play along with the music flowing through her headphones. Noting some residual uneasiness, Quincy kept up his banter from the board; when she spontaneously tapped the tambourine on her rear end, he cracked,

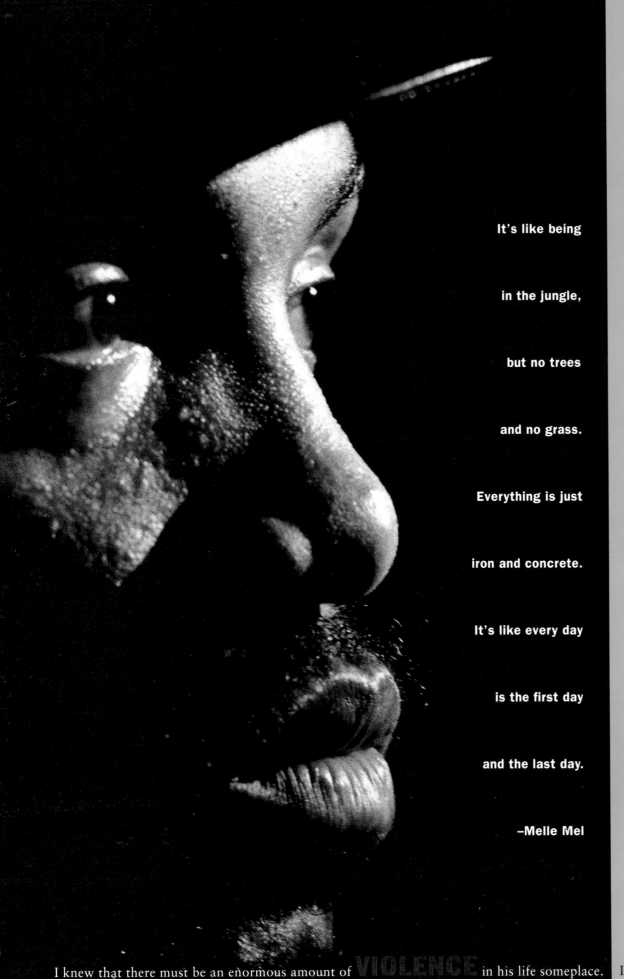

It's like being

in the jungle,

but no trees

and no grass.

Everything is just

iron and concrete.

It's like every day

is the first day

and the last day.

—Melle Mel

"Whoa, I like that sound!" After five or six passes he abruptly stopped her mid-take and went back into the studio. Gently taking the tambourine himself, he began to play it—and play it well. He showed her how to get more of a sixteenth-note feel, how to get exactly the rhythm he wanted. Then, back in the control room, he listened as she reproduced the part perfectly. The track was done.

Even in coaching a bit player, there had been not one note of condescension, no meanness or frustration. It was a perfect example of what Quincy has always done better than anyone else in the business: he uses his vast musical knowledge and his equally vast charm to get the best out of others, on the spot.

When today's pop fans think of Quincy Jones, they focus on his recent work with such stars as Michael Jackson, the Brothers Johnson, Frank Sinatra, James Ingram, Chaka Khan. For much of his half-century musical career, however, Quincy Jones has been associated with jazz, first as a trumpeter, then as an arranger. Many thought him the natural heir to the masters of the big-band idiom, Duke Ellington and Count Basie. In fact, he still uses arranging techniques learned while touring with those jazz geniuses. He creates sounds reminiscent of the unamplified interplay of the big bands' brass and reeds, but his chief tools today are electronic instruments intricately meshed through state-of-the-art computer technology. Matching old with new, bringing decades together in one unified sound, Quincy Jones's music bridges the distance between the dance floors of the fifties and the sound stages and control rooms of the eighties and nineties. For proof, you need only dip into his latest album, *Back on the Block*.

I knew that there must be an enormous amount of VIOLENCE in his life someplace. It's there in that score! —Sidney Lumet on *The Pawnbroker*

When you come out of Chicago for ten years...nothing is gonna surprise you. You see everything. –Quincy

On the way to school one day when we were six or seven, we stopped and saw this guy hanging by the back of his coat on the first rung of a telephone pole, with an ice pick stuck through his neck. We checked that out and went right on to school. –Lloyd Jones

Quincy Jones's accomplishments trace the course of popular and commercial music itself in the second half of the twentieth century. His writing and arranging credits from the fifties include albums and live appearances with Dizzy Gillespie, Dinah Washington, Ray Charles, Clifford Brown, Ella Fitzgerald, Billy Eckstine, Chuck Willis, Lionel Hampton, and a legion of other jazz giants. He arranged the brilliant *Sinatra: Live in Las Vegas at the Sands*, featuring the Count Basie Orchestra. *Newport 1961*, *This Is How I Feel about Jazz,* and *Birth of a Band* were three of the last great acoustic big-band

JOE LOUIS, 1937

efforts. Among his thirty-plus film scores are the tensely memorable soundtracks for *The Pawnbroker, In Cold Blood,* and *In the Heat of the Night.* For television he composed the strutting *Sanford and Son* and brassy *Ironside* themes, as well as the majestic music for the mini-series *Roots.* He pioneered as a composer and gambled as a producer; it was Quincy Jones who discovered the unknown Lesley Gore in 1963 and with "It's My Party," "You Don't Own Me," and "Judy's Turn to Cry" invented soap-opera ▶ PG 17

Daddy had taken Lloyd and me to one of Joe Louis's fights. And Joe Louis gave

It was me, Melle Mel, Kane,

us the boxing gloves that he won with. Waymond, who lived down the street,

and Quincy said, "Any one of us

had a BB gun, and I really wanted it bad. So I said, "I'll

in this room, twenty

trade you these boxing gloves for this BB gun!" Well, I

seconds in the other

went home, and my daddy was mad. He went back to

direction, we'd have been in

retrieve the gloves, and when he came back he was in love with Waymond's

the penitentiary, man." —Ice-T

mother, Elvira. She became my stepmother. —Quincy

*The greatest contribution
that my dad made was*
getting us out of Chicago.
—Lloyd Jones

We had just **one bedroom**,
a living space, and a kitchen.
Ten people in two rooms...

Katherine, *who's my stepsister...*

and my brother, Lloyd...

Waymond... *who's my half brother...*

and Margie, *who's my half sister...*

Willie Lee, Theresa...

BREMERTON, WASHINGTON, 1944

16

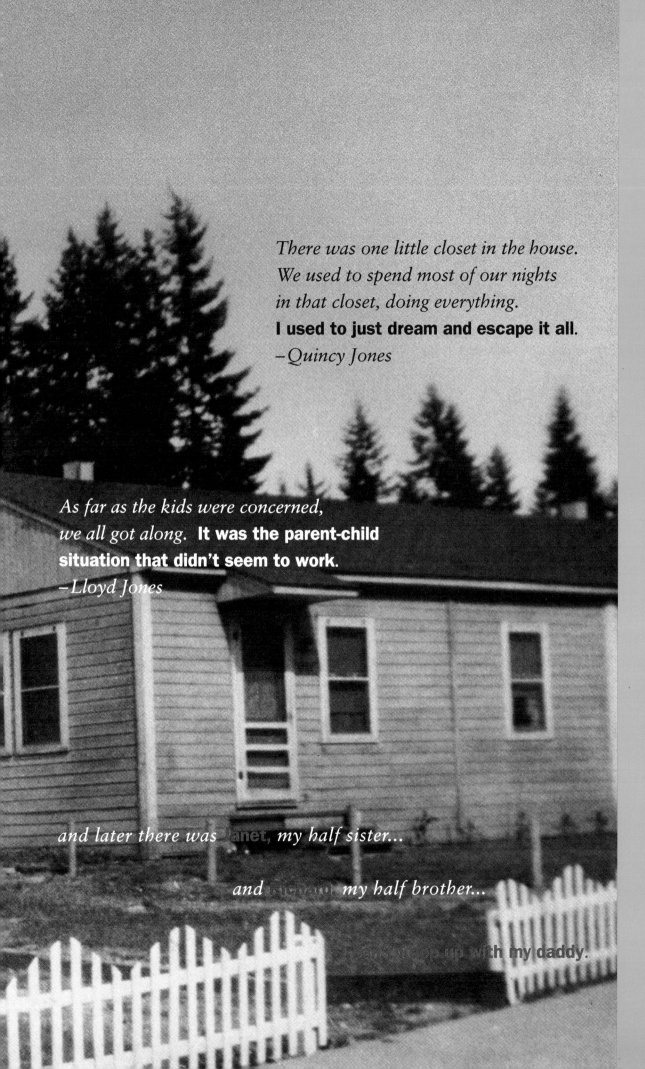

There was one little closet in the house. We used to spend most of our nights in that closet, doing everything. **I used to just dream and escape it all.**
—Quincy Jones

As far as the kids were concerned, we all got along. **It was the parent-child situation that didn't seem to work.**
—Lloyd Jones

and later there was Janet, my half sister...

and Theresa my half brother...

can't keep up with my daddy.

pop. In the seventies and eighties he created a classy string of technically assured funk-influenced pop albums for the Brothers Johnson, Rufus and Chaka Khan, George Benson, and James Ingram. His own solo album, *The Dude*, won multiple Grammys in 1981. The eighties also saw his epochal efforts with Michael Jackson, capped by *Thriller* (merely the best-selling pop record of all time) and the historic single "We Are the World." In 1985 Quincy's role in the filming of Alice Walker's *The Color Purple* marked the start of yet another career, film making.

What kind of man is Quincy Jones? One who lives in the car-mania capital of the world, Los Angeles, and doesn't drive; one who still has that cool, hip quality of a bebop veteran; one who uses words like "cat" and "man," notices pretty women, and makes city-kid comments about hanging out on the street. He is "Q" to his friends, and his youthful vitality, tempered by wisdom acquired the hard way, is implicit in every note of his music, be it bebop, big band, film score, or pop. That breathtaking immediacy in the vocals, the distinct presence of individual instruments, the warmth and grit in the rhythms, all bear Quincy's distinctive signature. The music is clean but never sterile or generic; he carefully weaves elements—instruments, voices, riffs, details—without ever forgetting where the focus should be. The sound of the artists—whether an ensemble of superstars or a lone clarinet—comes through clearly and crisply.

Quincy Jones is in his fifth decade as a working professional; along with Miles Davis, he is the only survivor of the bebop era who has stayed contemporary and continued to have an impact on today's music. Almost every other musician who still performs after a half-century on the road does so as a kind of living museum piece, rehearsing great music of the past for the nostalgic reverie of aging listeners. Quincy Jones is that rare musician who has grown and established a following among each new generation of listeners. Now in his late fifties, Quincy is better known and more influential, both as musician and businessman, than at any other time in his distinguished career. From bebop to rap, from soul to film scores, he's done just about everything a musician can in American popular music except stand still.

The evening of the 1982 Grammy Awards was truly a night of triumph for Jones. Center stage with Michael Jackson, basking in the glow of the record-breaking *Thriller*, he earned eight

QUINCY AS PRESIDENT OF BOYS CLUB, BREMERTON JR HIGH, 1947

Grammys, including Producer of the Year (shared with the artist he nicknamed "Smelly"). Television viewers around the world responded to the devilishly charming smile that had seduced so many collaborators into extraordinary performances, and celebrated with him.

Other triumphs have come in other, very different, fashions over the decades. In the seventies, Quincy schooled two young funk-playing Afroed brothers named George and Louis Johnson in their streetwise manner. In the sixties, Quincy wore a tux to conduct Sinatra and the

A white dude named Robin Fields said,

"Why don't you run for Boys' Club

IF JUST ONE PERSON BELIEVES IN YOU,

president, and I'll be your manager?"

"You gotta

THEN THE RESPONSIBILITY ISN'T ONLY

be joking!

There's twenty-eight

TO YOURSELF,

hundred kids and maybe thirty black

people here." He said, **"Let's do it."**

IT'S TO ANOTHER PERSON. –QUINCY

And I won. –Quincy

I was about fourteen the first time I went

to jail. And boy, that process was not fun!

The cops stopped us.

They saw five black

dudes in the car, and

Well, once **music** *grabbed my mind,*

they pulled us over.

I didn't want to blow my energy

They smelled the stuff

on all that dumb stuff anymore. —Quincy

and we were the headlines on the

***Bremerton Sun* the next day. —Quincy**

Basie Band for a well-heeled Vegas audience. In the fifties, he rehearsed five greasy-haired singers known as the Treniers in a Manhattan recording studio. One decade earlier, Quincy was in Seattle, Washington, in a small, crowded club, pungent with the smell of unfiltered cigarettes, raw liquor, and honeysuckle-sweet perfume. On the Brewington Elks Lounge bandstand, young cats in big-shouldered suits vamped on "Sophisticated Lady"; folks called their spinning solos and chords bebop. And right next to the piano player—a frisky left-hander named Ray

QUINCY IN HIGH SCHOOL BAND
(2ND ROW, 3RD FROM RIGHT), C. 1947

Charles—a slight, handsome trumpeter with a thin mustache sat on a wooden chair fingering his axe. The tip of his tongue nervously tapped his upper lip as he listened hard to the music floating above him. He got the nod, placed lip to mouthpiece, filled his lungs, and let loose the sounds running madly through his head.

That solo meant as much to Quincy Jones as the multiple Grammys would forty years later. He knew that sticking close to the big boys was the only way to learn their music. We've all profited from the education he received. ▶ PG 24

To get out of whatever was distasteful or

My daddy did the best he could, you know?

unpleasant or uncomfortable or painful–

He always encouraged whatever I was into.

music could always soothe that. You just

There were so many kids,

crawl in that  world and

reach in that black hole

and I wanted a music book in

and grab something beautiful, and it would

Bremerton, and it cost 98 cents or something, and he

take you away from all of that.

would sneak the money to me,

because he didn't have enough to give to everybody.

A Composer's Dream

Any composer would hope to dream,
of a song that would shock the world.
A song that would make them peak up their ears.
And listen to his music unfurl

A song should have all the beauty,
and the color of every rose.
with a tree for every note and rest
the music that the people will know.

A composer's ideas are part of his heart
they're just on paper to be played
he works to be ready on the final day
when his can make your ears, his maid

Surely, this was the idea of Beethoven
Bach, Chopin and ~~████~~ Ravel
But as the years roll on and farther
Their ideas we can never tell

But as a composer dreams on and on
and his dreams are hopeless it seems
Even if the people don't listen
He can always thank god for his dreams.

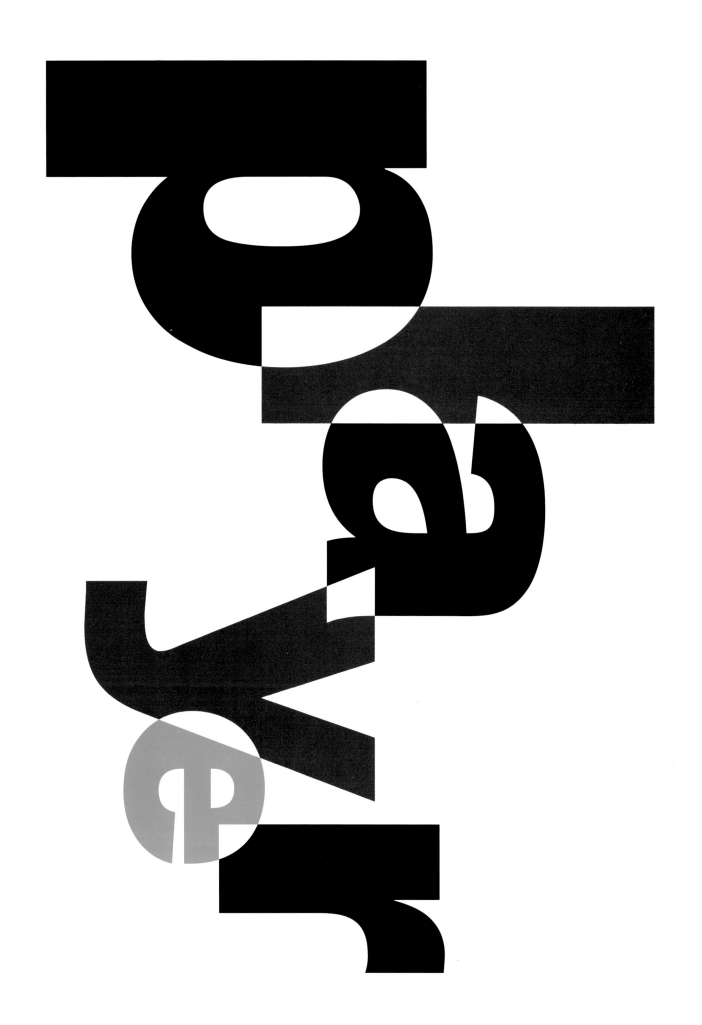

The nervous neophyte developed into a man who calls Sinatra and Melle Mel his pals, and whose praises are sung by Barbra Streisand, Michael Jackson, Steven Spielberg, Oprah Winfrey, Lionel Richie, and Jesse Jackson. But Quincy didn't begin with any advantages or many friends—far from it. His was a long and arduous trip that began on the hard streets of Chicago, Illinois.

Beginnings of a Native Son

Throughout the long, dark years before and during the Civil War, the boldest of the African-American slaves had sought their freedom by escaping "up North." In the twentieth century, a second great migration of African-Americans took place, as papers like the *Chicago Defender* and the *Pittsburgh Courier* waged a campaign to fill factories in the burgeoning industrial cities with black laborers. Liberation and freedom, the papers said, could be tasted in New York, Philadelphia, Detroit, and Chicago, and throughout the twenties and thirties, family after family left their Southern homes to come north.

Quincy Delight Jones, Senior, came to Chicago from South Carolina to work as a carpenter (and semi-pro baseball player). His wife, Sarah, whom he had met and married in Chicago, came from Mississippi. On March 14, 1933, Quincy Delight Jones, Junior, was born.

1933–1943: Chicago, Joe Louis, Lucy Jackson

Quincy's parents had come to Chicago hoping just to find a decent living and the human rights denied them in the segregated South. In 1945, in his introduction to *Black Metropolis*, the distinguished sociological survey of the migration to Chicago, Richard Wright (who had come from Mississippi in the thirties) wrote eloquently of the appearance of Chicago, "that great iron city, that impersonal, mechanical city, amid the steam, the smoke, the snowy winds, the blister-

MILES DAVIS, 1989

ing suns … Many migrants like us were driven and pursued, in the manner of characters in a Greek play, down the paths of defeat; but luck must have been with us, for we somehow survived."

Quincy, Senior, and Sarah had heard that Chicago was developing a reputation for black entrepreneurial opportunities. They didn't expect paradise, but devastating personal events kept them from enjoying even a modest, stable home. Sarah Jones began to suffer from chronic mental illness, and for most of young Quincy's childhood, his mother was either under a doctor's close care or in an institution. Quincy and his younger brother, Lloyd, saw her so infrequently that years later Quincy would say, "I never knew what it was like to have a mother."

Even without such family trauma, city life was harsh and unpromising for young black boys in the Depression. The enticing promises of newspapers notwithstanding, black families found their prospects curtailed by segregation and poverty as devastating in its urban incarnation, on Chicago's ill-kept South Side, as it had been in the rural South. Hemmed in on all sides, excluded from decent schools or jobs, black youngsters sought ways to break loose.

Some, like the protagonist of Wright's *Native Son,* vented their frustration in bloody bouts of violence; street fighting was commonplace in the black ghetto. Quincy recalls witnessing as a child many ghastly knifings and shootings around his own neighborhood, a typical one on the South Side where most of the black migrants clustered. Some kids funneled their anxiety and energy into sports, and, in particular, into boxing, which was the most financially rewarding enterprise for minority athletes at the time. The Brown Bomber, heavyweight champion Joe Louis, lived in Quincy's neighborhood and was an acquaintance of Quincy, Senior. Louis's powerful presence made a profound impression on the youngster. Years later, Quincy arranged the jazz ▶ PG 28

C_{harlie Parker}

Charlie Parker was one of the most important geniuses of the twentieth century.

He had it all, the perfect balance of really understanding what the technical side of the instrument is about—he could play anything—and this soul on top of it.

We still haven't caught up to him yet. He was absolutely the greatest improviser I ever heard in my life.

One thing I miss now when I listen to records is "Holy shit, what was that?" I used to get that from Clifford Brown and from Dizzy: "What is that? What are they doing!" When you hear things that are happening now, and you like it, you never say, "Man, what are they doing!" Because you know what they're doing.

I miss that boldness, that kind of force that just crashes through your psyche like that. I think you ought to leave fugue and counterpoint alone after Bach and find something else to do with your time. Because this man was a genius guided by God, and that's what Charlie Parker was. –Q

And the moment I heard Bird, I said, **YEAH,** *that's how music should sound.* –Dizzy Gillespie

In SEATTLE we were fortunate enough to run into a bunch of energetic kids who really wanted to PLAY.

—Bobby Tucker

He asked me to show

him how to do...

how to write this

or how to write that.

—Ray Charles

So he said, "But the only time

I could do it would be

before I go to school in the morning."

I said, "Oh, what time is that?"

He said, "Like about six, six thirty." —Clark Terry

We were so thrilled to be playing with Billie Holiday–we were kids–that we forgot to turn the music sheets over. I remember

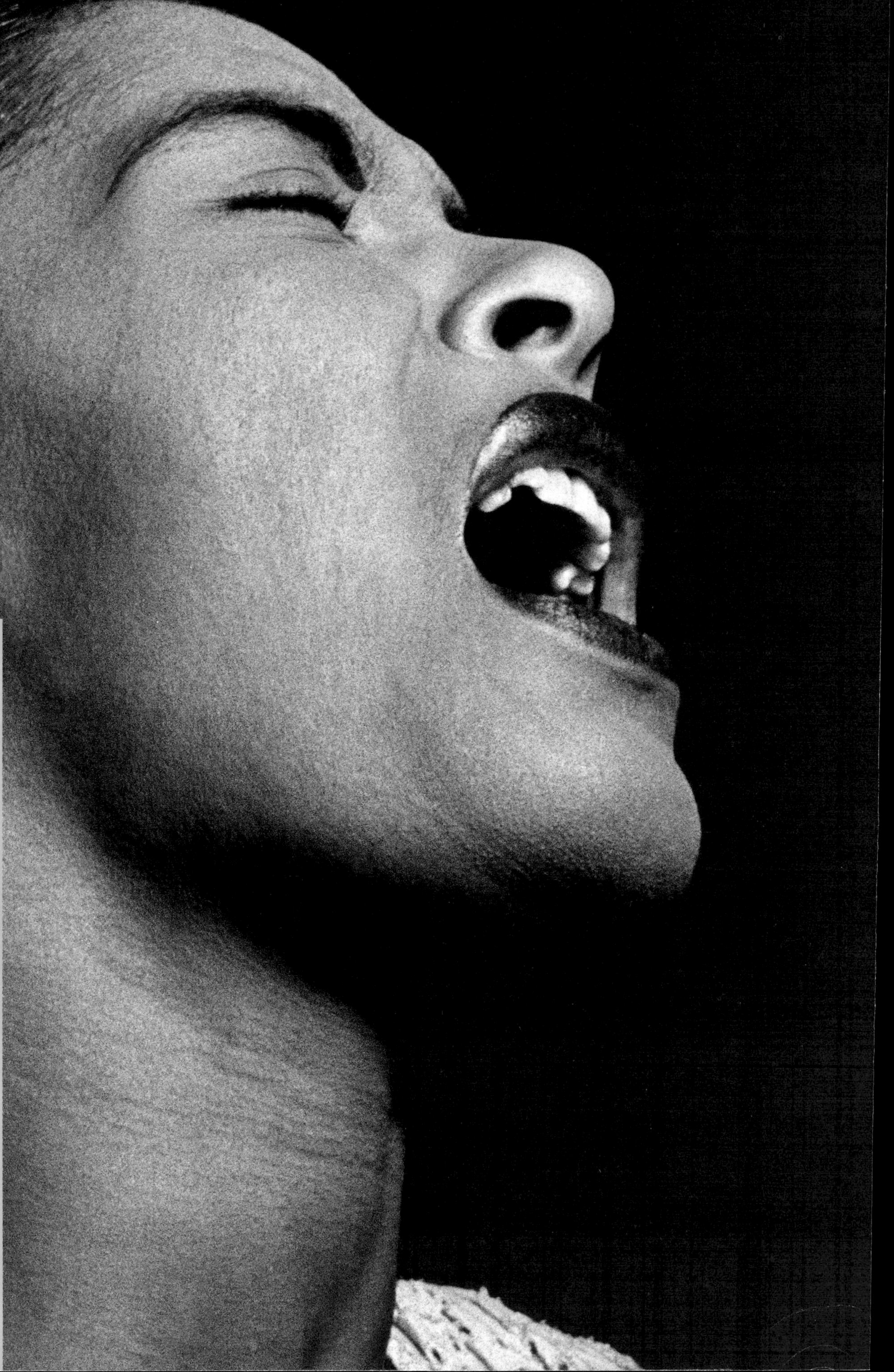

standard "Killer Joe" as a tribute to Louis's excellence.

In that environment of chaos, though, a new and more profound influence came over Quincy: music entered his life through a brick wall. Lucy Jackson, a child who lived next door, took piano lessons every week, and Quincy would sit in his house during the day, listening as her fingers pressed the keys and her feet pushed the pedals. In the era of the ubiquitous boom box and portable CD player, it's difficult perhaps for a young person to imagine the impact a single unamplified piano could have, but before stereo, before transistor radios even, the piano's 88 keys produced a rich sound that, for Quincy, was magic itself.

That burst of music from Lucy Jackson's piano would resonate throughout Quincy's life, but as it turned out, there would be little time to think much about music in Chicago. Quincy

Bobby Tucker saying, "Come on, guys, I'm gonna make you buy a ticket in a minute." *Because we were in awe of this woman.* –Quincy

WALKER
H
NIGHTLY

BUMPS BLACKWELL JUNIOR BAND
SEATTLE C. 1949, QUINCY AT LEFT

and his brother were having their hair cut one afternoon in 1943 when their father arrived with their luggage packed and Trailways bus tickets in his hand. They were heading west. Destination? The state of Washington. Purpose? A new job.

1943–1951: Seattle, YMCA Debut, Ray Charles, Clark Terry

One of World War II's untold stories is the impact of that conflict on black migration and family life. Southern segregation and racism had driven blacks north, and the economic prejudices and continued segregation they found there sent many families out West, where racial lines weren't as rigid and jobs were available in factories supporting the war effort. In Oakland, Compton, and other less celebrated Western cities, new migrants sought another start. ▶ PG 34

'Be-Bop

DIZZY GILLESPIE, 1948
FLAVOR FLAV, 1989

I see a connection between **Hip Hop** *and* **Be-Bop.** *They both had to invent their own language.* *You know,* **"IF YOU DON'T LET US IN YOUR CULTURE, THEN WE'LL START OUR OWN!" —QUINCY**

DIZZY GILLESPIE

MY ROLLING STONES

I think Betty Carter told me about Quincy.

AND BEATLES ARE

She said, "There's this young trumpet player...

DIZZY GILLESPIE

Writes his ass off."

AND MILES DAVIS.

I think we had some of the same girlfriends, too. –Miles Davis

–QUINCY

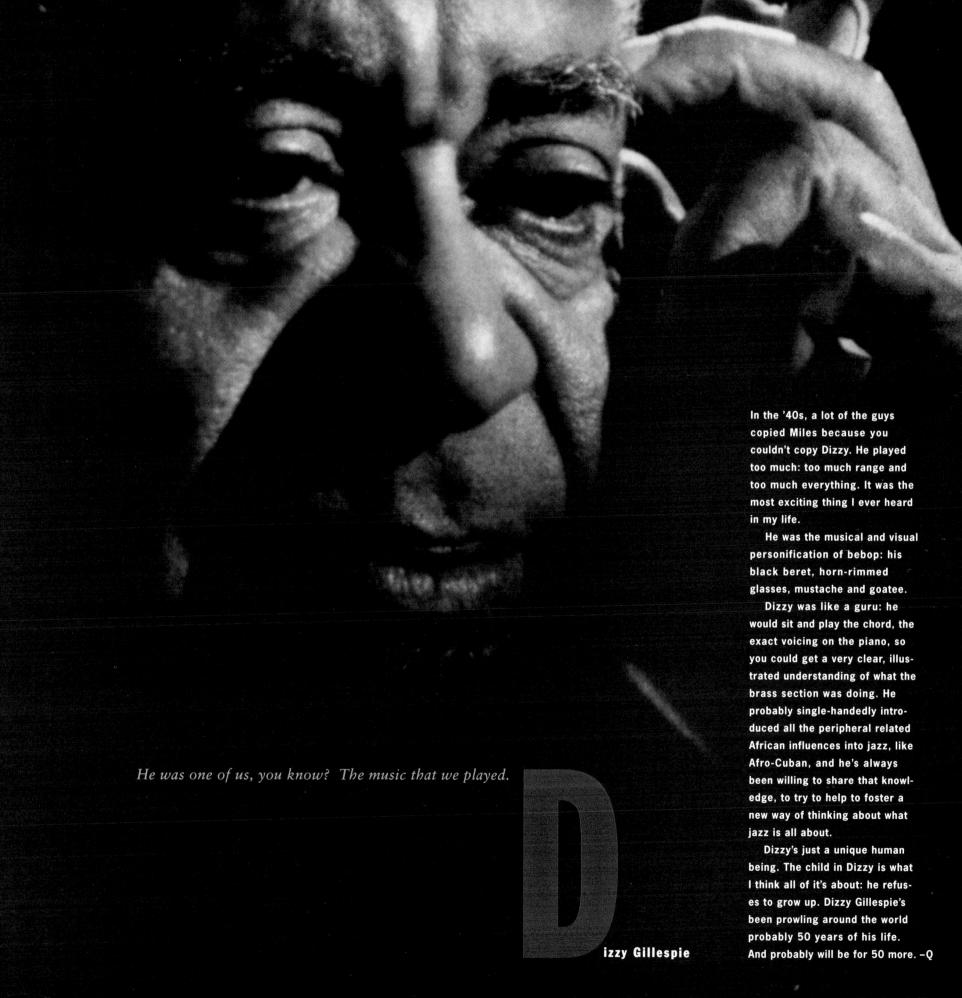

He was one of us, you know? The music that we played.

Dizzy Gillespie

In the '40s, a lot of the guys copied Miles because you couldn't copy Dizzy. He played too much: too much range and too much everything. It was the most exciting thing I ever heard in my life.

He was the musical and visual personification of bebop: his black beret, horn-rimmed glasses, mustache and goatee.

Dizzy was like a guru: he would sit and play the chord, the exact voicing on the piano, so you could get a very clear, illustrated understanding of what the brass section was doing. He probably single-handedly introduced all the peripheral related African influences into jazz, like Afro-Cuban, and he's always been willing to share that knowledge, to try to help to foster a new way of thinking about what jazz is all about.

Dizzy's just a unique human being. The child in Dizzy is what I think all of it's about: he refuses to grow up. Dizzy Gillespie's been prowling around the world probably 50 years of his life. And probably will be for 50 more. –Q

Bremerton was one of these towns, and on July 4, 1943, Quincy, his father, his brother Lloyd, his stepmother Elvira, and her three children arrived in a bright new world.

"My father got a job at the Bremerton Shipyards, run by the navy," remembers Quincy. "We lived in a place way out of town, way up on a hill called Sinclair Heights. It was the black section of the city. If you were a brother, that's where you lived." While it was hardly an integrated paradise, it was a lot less dangerous and obviously oppressive than Chicago. "You had to walk three miles up that hill. It was like a ghetto project, but it was all new and it looked so good!"

Freed of fear on the street, Quincy turned into an enterprising adolescent, willing to work hard at almost anything to earn money. His jobs included shining shoes, babysitting, picking strawberries, delivering newspapers, washing windows, working in a dry cleaners, and, in a job that may have given him his ear for crescendos, setting pins in a bowling alley.

IT WASN'T LIKE

I was really ready to work.

When I was eleven I got a job

steam pressing clothes...

He'd say, "Go pick up the clothes!"

BEIN' NEUTRAL.

And I used to watch him press,

you know? I said,

"Well, I can do that!" – Quincy

GOING BACKWARDS.

I used to shine shoes for pimps...take bleach with the toothbrush

and go real easy around the side of the shoes.

All the pimps loved the way I used to do that.

WAS IMPOSSIBLE. –QUINCY

STANDING STILL WAS

"I see you got a trumpet in your hand, there.

Can you play trumpet?" And he said, "Sure I can!" I said,

"I'd like for you to come and go to Portland with the band." – Lionel Hampton

STANDING STILL WAS

I was fifteen...I got on this bus

and waited for four hours...

STANDING STILL

and finally the band got on the bus

and Gladys Hampton said,

"Get that child off the bus!

Go back to school!"

I was really torn up. –Quincy

Quincy's move from listening to playing music was instigated by a most unlikely person: his barber. Barbershops have always been more than just places to get a haircut. They also serve as unofficial men's clubs, where useful folk wisdom and macho bluster flow freely over the sound of clippers. Eddie Lewis, the proprietor of the Sinclair Heights Barbershop, used his hands to grease up processed hair, trim mustaches, and, when he wasn't too busy, play the trumpet.

Twelve-year-old Quincy, hanging around the shop when he wasn't hustling a new job, was fascinated by the range of sounds that came out of Lewis's instrument. Soon music had replaced all of Quincy's other, more profitable, extracurricular activities. He was determined to make a go of it on one instrument or another. He joined the school band and tried his hand at snare drum, bass drum, and timpani; he put his lips to sousaphone, B-flat baritone and E-flat alto sax, and French horn, but he spent the most time wrestling with the mysteries of the trumpet mouthpiece. In 1947, Quincy Jones made his professional ▶ PG 38

I asked Ray,

"Well, what does the

brass section play?

They're playing all

those **HOT** licks,

but everybody's

playing different notes.

What are they doing?"

And he said nothing

and he just hit a

root position,

B-flat-seventh,

and on top of that

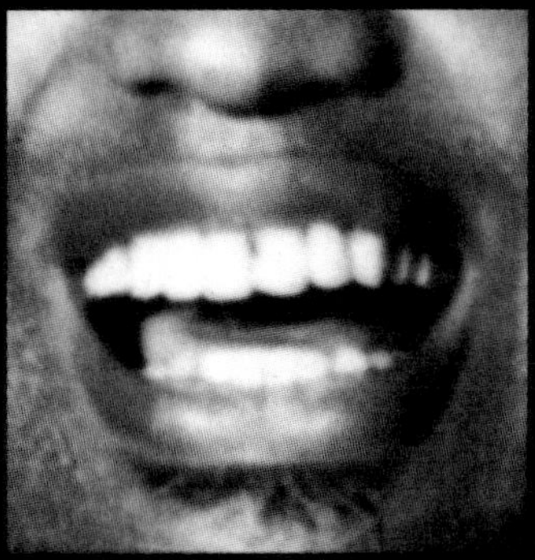

put a C-seventh.

Eight notes. And it was

like ... **ZOOM**,

a hyperspace kind of

a revelation just came

into my mind and it

opened up a whole

door to a wonder

world...a wonder

world I've been

in **LOVE** with

ever since.

—Quincy

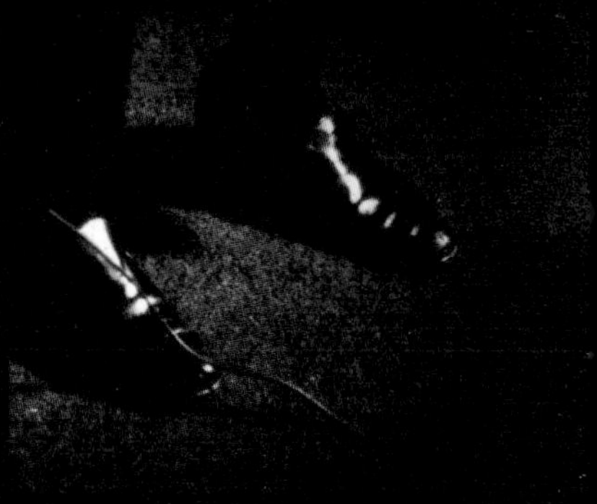

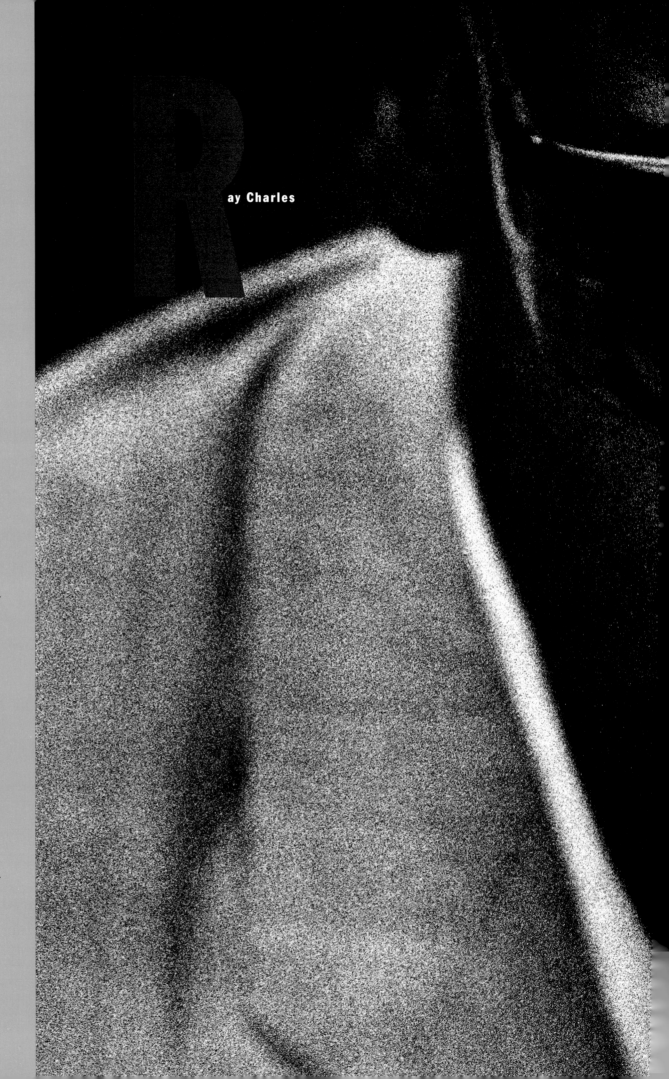

ay Charles

debut, earning seven dollars for an appearance with an unnamed band at the Bremerton YMCA.

Music quickly moved from pastime to obsession for Quincy. Luckily for him, all the great black entertainers came through town sooner or later; Seattle was a port city, filled with black men and women who, like Quincy, Senior, had found work in the wartime factories, and the music tour organizers knew they'd find ready audiences if they followed the workers' trail. Stars passing through town could tell the boy had been hit badly with a musical bug. "He couldn't have been any more than thirteen years old at the time, and would always hustle his way into shows by carrying someone's axe," Billy Eckstine remembers. "Through rehearsal and every set during our stand in town he would sit right in front of the bandstand with his big eyes and just watch—never said a word—just watched and smiled. I remember seeing his eyes glued on the trumpet section, or the piano player. During the breaks he'd study all the arrangements, memorizing parts, asking the various arrangers how they did this or why they wrote that. His need for knowledge at such a young age was really something to see, and because he was so damn inquisitive, everybody in the band tried to give him some help." It wasn't just curiosity that drew Quincy in; the boy was sharp enough to realize that the musical education he needed was waiting for him backstage. Swing was on its way out, and something called rhythm and blues began to take its place as the prevailing black dance music. While we tend to think of the South as the spawning ground for early R&B, the West Coast also played a crucial role. Two pioneers in the Seattle area itself—Bumps Blackwell and Ray Charles— came to have considerable influence over fourteen-year-old Quincy Jones when his family moved from Bremerton to nearby Seattle in 1947.

Bumps Blackwell, who later masterminded the early hits of Little Richard and Sam Cooke, was a bandleader whose gigs took him all ▶ PG 47

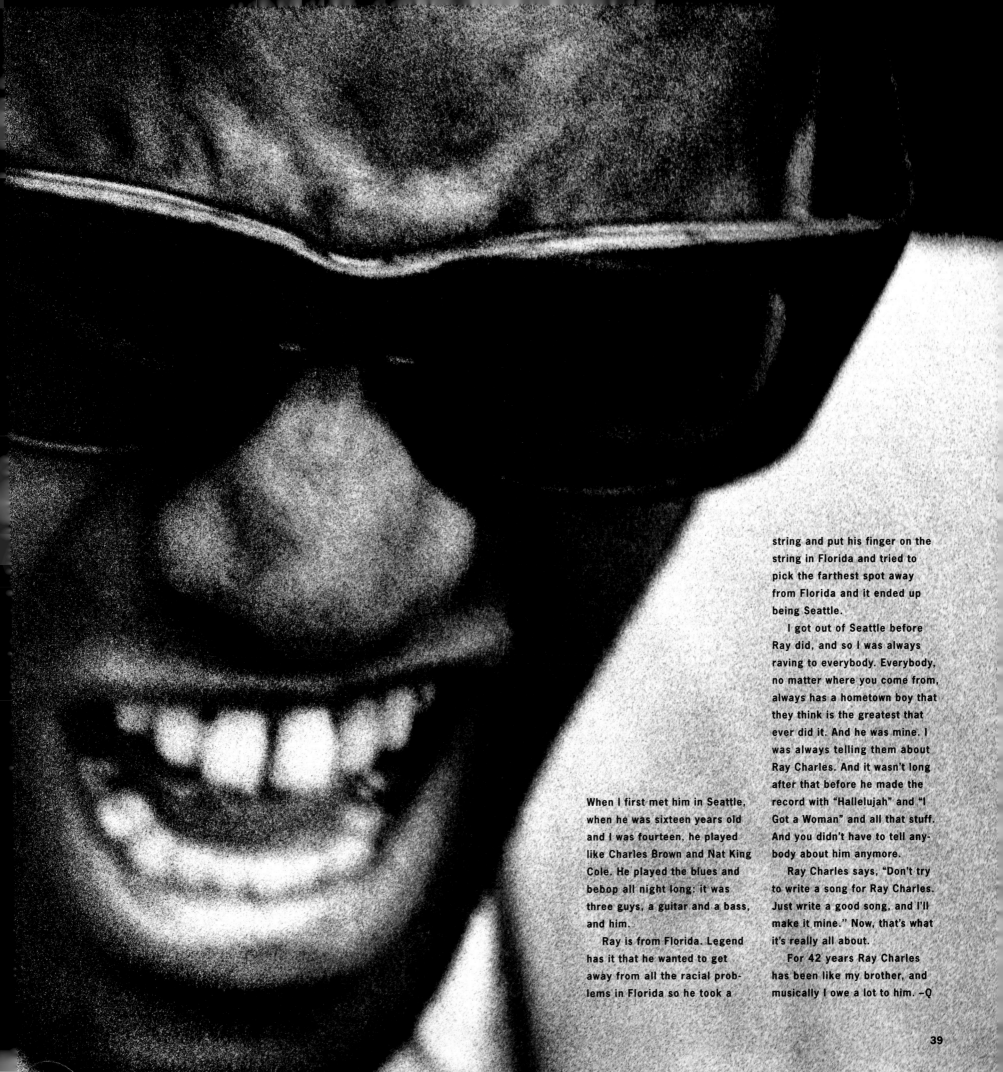

When I first met him in Seattle, when he was sixteen years old and I was fourteen, he played like Charles Brown and Nat King Cole. He played the blues and bebop all night long; it was three guys, a guitar and a bass, and him.

Ray is from Florida. Legend has it that he wanted to get away from all the racial problems in Florida so he took a string and put his finger on the string in Florida and tried to pick the farthest spot away from Florida and it ended up being Seattle.

I got out of Seattle before Ray did, and so I was always raving to everybody. Everybody, no matter where you come from, always has a hometown boy that they think is the greatest that ever did it. And he was mine. I was always telling them about Ray Charles. And it wasn't long after that before he made the record with "Hallelujah" and "I Got a Woman" and all that stuff. And you didn't have to tell anybody about him anymore.

Ray Charles says, "Don't try to write a song for Ray Charles. Just write a good song, and I'll make it mine." Now, that's what it's really all about.

For 42 years Ray Charles has been like my brother, and musically I owe a lot to him. –Q

JOE GORDON, EV PERRY, DIZZY GILLESPIE,
CARL WARWICK, QUINCY, BIRDLAND, 1949

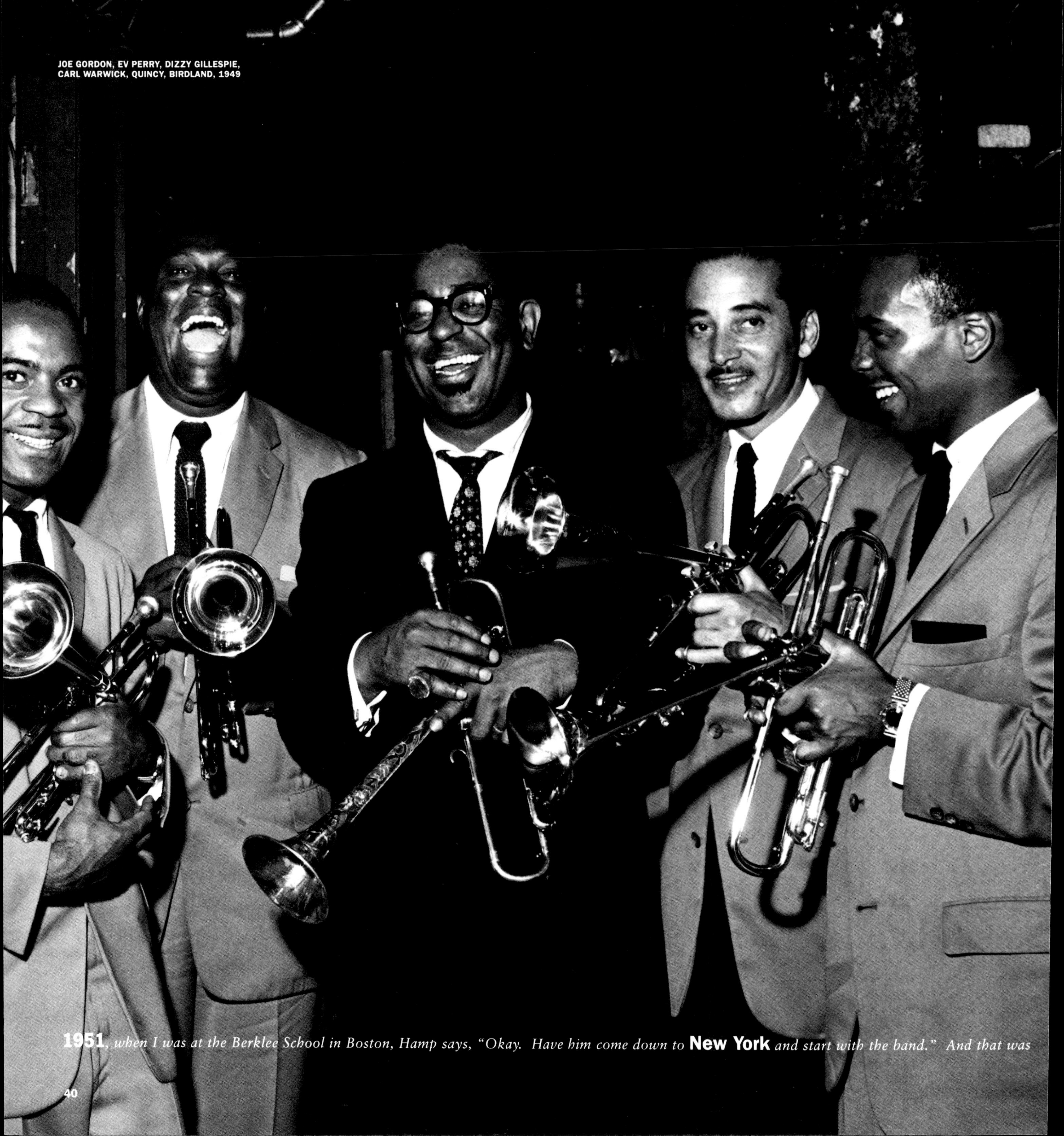

1951, *when I was at the Berklee School in Boston, Hamp says, "Okay. Have him come down to* **New York** *and start with the band." And that was*

one of the happiest moments ever in my life...You talk about first big breaks, that was it. **Birdland** *was the first place I*

41

Clark Terry

I met Clark Terry in Seattle when I was 13, when he was with Count Basie's small band. I used to just sit there all day and listen to every show they did. I had never heard a trumpet player in my life like Clark. I still haven't.

Clark has got that burnished, brass sound. It's a warm tone, but with a fluidity that's almost like a saxophone. And it's mixed with an enormous wit. You know, he's a funny dude—he sees funny images all the time and that comes through in his music. Like his tune "Mumbles."

He was my teacher, although teaching is a funny word, because part of the teaching process is sitting there every show and watching Clark play. I used to bug him to death when he'd try to relax and party—I was always just trying to get him to talk about the trumpet, talk about music, talk about the East Coast, talk about how you play and stuff; I was a stone CB.

Clark had worked in a circus band—they didn't have a lot of money for the band, so the trumpet player had to take a sock cymbal and keep time with his foot while he was playing his trumpet. It's no accident that Clark was a major influence on Miles Davis. They were both from East St. Louis.

One of the biggest thrills of my life was when Clark Terry and Quentin Jackson left the Duke Ellington band to join my big band in Paris for the Free and Easy Tour. –Q

"Quincy was a **tremendous**

jazz trumpet player." – Lionel Hampton

"He wasn't that good a trumpet player."

–Bobby Tucker

"Turned out to be a

marvelous

trumpet player." – Clark Terry

"He was a horrible

trumpet player." – Billy Eckstine

My mother and I were somewhere

waiting for him in a restaurant...

but he never showed up.

I used to say to her,

"Well, I don't know why

we're waiting, he's not gonna come!"

We just thought he had

this genius in him and

IT HAD TO BE.

Everything else was second,

which wasn't so right for us,

but that's how it was.

—Jolie Jones Levine

It was all about saving
in whatever areas they could.
Not going to the movies,
not having babysitters,
so that my father could go
down to wherever he had to go
to be with the right people,
to get where he wanted to go.

JERI AND JOLIE, 1960

44

My first baby. And I was crazy. I was a baby myself. —*Quincy*

It was an interracial marriage

QUINCY AND JERI, PARIS 1960

My first wife was from high school. We met at 15. And she moved to New York when I was about 19 and I had a child, **Jolie**.

at a time when that was not

the happening thing.

—Jolie Jones Levine

ionel Hampton

Lionel's band was like my dream, the dream band to be with. They would come to Seattle and it was like the invasion of Normandy.

Hamp is an incredible musician, an incredible vibes player—he'd play "Moonglow" and some of those ballads and make your eyes cross he could play so well.

What made him such a good vibe player was that he was a drummer first. And brought a great rhythmic feel to his melodic concept.

The band was designed to have the full range of music and entertainment. And serious show business. To me, Hamp was the first rock and roll band. There's no question about it—it's the first band I ever heard that was concerned with having a big funky beat and really seduced an audience with a passion. And on top to the big beat he would drag in swing music, bebop, or whatever felt good.

Hamp was real serious about band meetings. After every performance there was a meeting. A meeting about anything. About music, about attitude, about show biz, about anything. As long as it was a meeting. He ran the emotional side of it and his wife, Gladys, ran the business side (she was like a mother to me). And he would call everybody Gates, nobody had a first name there. "I'm tellin' you, Gates, you gotta do this. Because I don't need any of you! I don't need anybody. I can do it all myself."

The alumni of Hamp's read like the who's who of jazz: Joe Newman, Illinois Jacquet, Fats Navarro, Monk Montgomery, Jerome Richardson, Jimmy Cleveland, Milt Buckner, it went on and on.

I remember playing one night at the Band Box [next door to Birdland] and Clifford Brown, Art Farmer, and myself were the trumpet section and Bird came in from next door and sat in with us reading the tenor sax parts for three sets. Morris Levy, the owner of Birdland, came in and had a fit since Bird was headlining next door.

Lionel Hampton's band was the best school any musician could ever dream of. And he was one happy young dude. –Q

across the Pacific Northwest. Insinuating himself and his trumpet into Blackwell's entourage, Quincy began to get real experience playing behind the stars traveling with the band, including legendary jazz vocalist Billie Holiday. Blackwell, like Jones, was a musician with many talents. "Bumps had a lot of jobs in Bremerton," Quincy recollects. "He had a butcher shop, he had a taxicab, he was an engineer at Boeing, he had a jewelry store, he had a big band, he had a senior eight-piece band and a junior eight-piece band that included Buddy Catlitt, Major Pigford, Howard Redmond, Oscar Holden, Floyd Standifer, and Billy Towles. Bumps was a real dude. He had a house there and we used to run around his house all the time."

Ray Charles was, in 1948, a worldly eighteen-year-old who'd recently moved to ▶ PG 51

It was a **GREAT** outfit.

–Lionel Hampton

We had a special outfit…Kind of purple shorts, and socks and shoes

and purple coats, and Tyrolean hats! He was gonna make us wear

this shit. When Hamp went upstairs, we followed behind him, and

standing there were *Miles, Charlie Mingus, Thelonious Monk, Bud*

Powell, Bird, all these hip dudes. Our idols, you know? You'd just

be dying of shame to let these guys see us wearing this kind of shit,

you know? So Clifford and I ran back down the steps and started to

act like we were tying our shoes. Because we couldn't do it. We were

too humiliated…You talk about conflict of styles. –Quincy

M

iles Davis

I met Miles at the Downbeat Club in New York. Somebody introduced me to him and he said, "I was listening to the radio before I came down, and I heard somebody trying to play like me."

And I was, I always tried to play like Miles.

Musically, Miles is a painter: it is like he slings snatches of scarlet and gold and chartreuse across a black canvas, in all sorts of interesting shapes. And with lots of economy—he knows the power of air and space, but every note is a perfect note, in the right spot, rhythmically and melodically.

Miles loves to give the impression of being this real tough callous person, always intimidating. But I never really bought into that, because I always listened to his records: there's that big soul in there that's crying! Really crying and with all that beauty, passion, and pain.

A lot of the bebop revolution was about, "I don't have to be an entertainer and a performer for the people, I want to be an artist first. I don't want to sing, I don't want to have to smile, I don't want to have to laugh."

It was about being hip, it was being cool. That's what Miles is about: flair and drama. –Q

Seattle from his native Florida. The pianist-vocalist was blind, but that didn't destroy his self-reliance. Still years away from the gospel-flavored hits he would record in the late fifties, Charles was building a reputation in the Pacific Northwest as a jazz improviser and crooner who appealed to the fans of Nat King Cole. His personal style attracted the young Jones, and the two began a friendship that continues to this day.

Charles remembers the budding trumpeter's thirst for real musical education. "Quincy was playing trumpet, but he really wanted to write jazz," says Charles. "So he asked me how to do it. I showed him my methods of arranging for big bands—I was doing a lot of that in Seattle—and he soaked it all up. Q was hungry for information, eager to learn anything he could. He was a sweet, likable dude. We ribbed each other a lot—still do—but that's 'cause there's love between us."

Quincy gives full credit to Charles for providing key lessons in arrangement. He told Alex Haley that it was Charles who "taught me how to read and write in Braille, and how to voice horns and how to deal with polytonality, and that opened up a golden door for me. I was fascinated with how all those instruments, each of them with its own distinctive sound, could play their own individual variations on the tune and yet interweave into the fabric of a song. From then on, I was hooked on the idea of orchestration and arranging."

But playing came first, and the teenager's nights were packed with music of every variety, from R&B to classic swing to hackneyed popular standards. "We played from seven till ten at the white clubs like the Seattle Tennis Club and fraternity houses at the University of Washington. Then we'd play from ten to about one or two in the morning at the Booker T. Washington Educational and Social Club and the Rocking Chair and the Black and Tan—all black clubs. At two or three, everybody would rush down to

DIZZY GILLESPIE

the Elks Club, where we'd play bebop all night long, till six or seven in the morning. That was the one that we didn't get paid for, but that's the one we all looked forward to—we got rid of all the just-making-a-living music, and went down to the Elks to play bebop. When people write about the music, jazz is in this box, R&B is in this box, pop is in this box. But we did everything— every night, man."

While still in Seattle, Quincy also made his first contact with two jazz giants who would serve as friends and mentors through his early years as a musician: Count Basie and his long-time star soloist, trumpeter Clark Terry. The relationship between the boy and the bandmen began quite casually. Quincy would just slip backstage with an instrument case under his arm, knowing that if he walked in briskly, he'd be mistaken for a band member and could mingle freely with them. Then that same enthusiasm ▶ PG 59

MILES DAVIS, BIRDLAND 1949

White people, American white people, successful white people, aren't familiar with the black man's culture. —Miles Davis

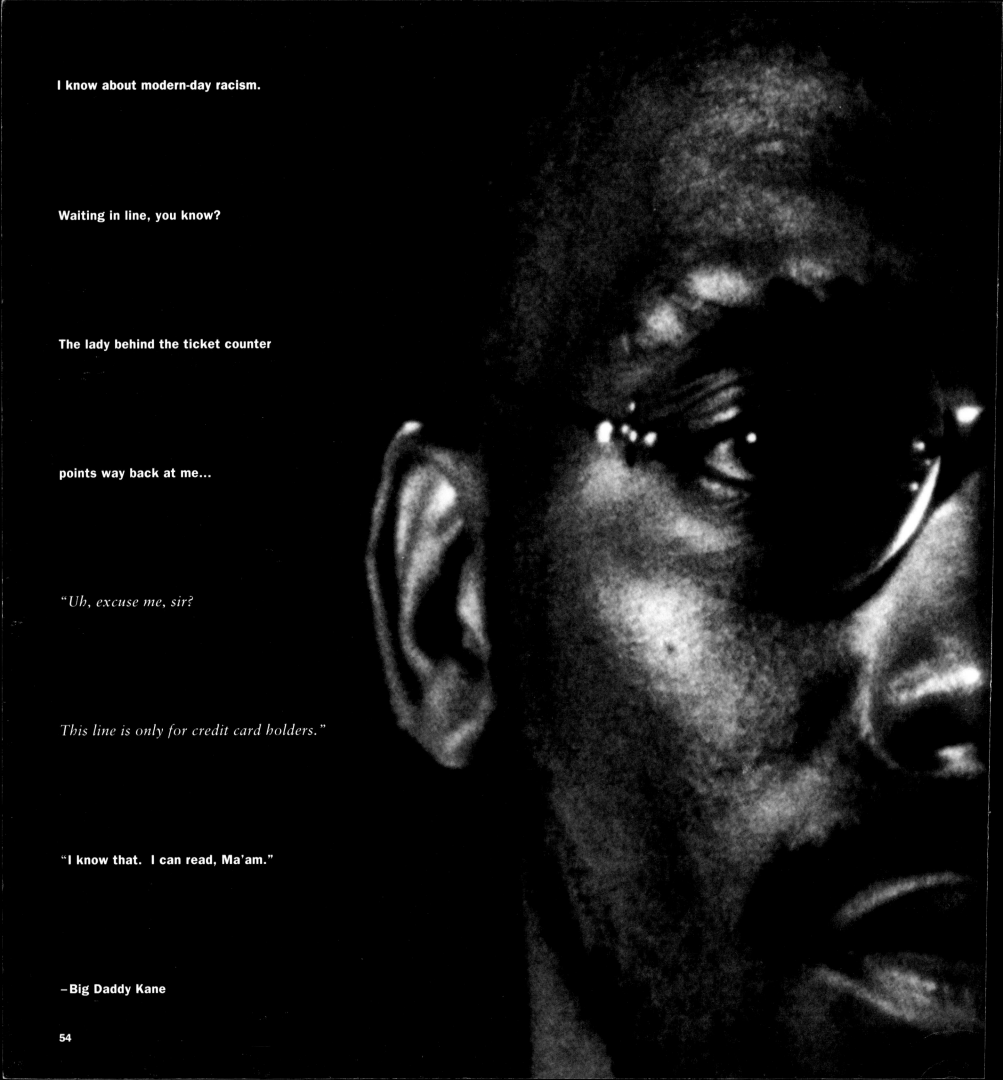

I know about modern-day racism.

Waiting in line, you know?

The lady behind the ticket counter

points way back at me...

"Uh, excuse me, sir?

This line is only for credit card holders."

"I know that. I can read, Ma'am."

–Big Daddy Kane

There's an **ATTITUDE** that you could just

Hamp would do seventy straight

smell. **You**

could almost

one-nighters in the Carolinas.

And we'd go through these little

just *taste* **it, you know. With the HATE** *stares,*

towns, and you know you were in...

and every-

thing else.

*almost like in **enemy** territory.*

It just...it just had a *smell* to it. –Quincy

"You know, I'm learning to write music, too. I'd like to see if you guys would play one of my arrangements." I said, "Yeah, sure!" So we

that had caught Billy Eckstine's eye would go to work for him again.

"At the time, Basie was the biggest and the best big-band leader in the world, but he took me under his wing. He was my uncle, my mentor, my friend—the dearest man in the world," Quincy says. "And his trumpet man, Clark Terry, practically adopted me. He taught me and talked to me and gave me the confidence to get out there and see what I could do on my own. These are the guys who really trained me; they were my idols as musicians, but even more important, they were my role models as human beings. They were more concerned about getting better than about getting over."

The education in arranging that Ray Charles had begun was now rounded out by Basie and Terry. Basie even used a couple of Quincy's arrangements in the show, a great compliment to the fifteen-year-old's talent. Arrangements were, at the time, crucial to any band's identity. Today producers are the kings, wielding technological batons over drum machines and synthesizers to create the desired effect; but for the large touring bands of the swing era, it was the arranger who had to give each new song or old standard a setup geared to the talents and idiosyncrasies of the particular players in that band. If Clark Terry, known for his aggressive attack and sturdy high notes, was playing with Basie that night, the arranger had to set a tempo that accentuated those strengths while charting passages that kept the rest of the horns and brass on their toes. He might offset strong unison playing with showcased solos. To the great arrangers, every instrument is a color; it's up to them to know which hue works best in the infinitely shifting combinations. By his seventeenth birthday, Quincy Jones had mastered the whole palette and had developed a sophisticated style that already commanded notice. ▶ PG 62

had a chance to run it down. "How'd you like it?" I said, "Oh, it was **fantastic!**" Actually it was **atrocious!** –Clark Terry

**DINAH WASHINGTON
REHEARSING WITH THE DELLS, 1961**

Quincy Jones is one of the best friends a song ever had! – Whitney Houston

Dinah

was so

beautiful to me.

She started

me out in the

record business.

—Quincy

The musical possibilities were enormous —bebop and swing, playing and arranging. Young Quincy did not need to choose a single direction yet, but he had recognized that Washington was not the place to grow as a player or an arranger. In 1950, he won a scholarship to the University of Seattle, but to reach further, he had to get out of Seattle. His ticket out was a scholarship to Boston's Schillinger House of Music (or Berklee College of Music, as it is now known). In the summer of 1951, Quincy and his young love, Jeri Caldwell, moved east. Boston, he knew, would only be a brief stop. New York, the home of bebop, was the real destination. It was the end of one apprenticeship and the start of another.

1951: The Big Apple, Bebop, Charlie Parker, Dizzy Gillespie, Lionel Hampton

Today, 1674 Broadway is the site of the Kit Kat Klub, a tacky bar where businessmen in white shirts and a few blue-jeaned workers throw back liquid lunches and ogle scantily clad hostesses. A few years back, it was a Latin club, where lover boys in white suits, shirts opened to display gold chains, danced with lovely ladies to the sound of salsa's 3/4 clave rhythm. In the sixties, it was the groovy discotheque Cheetah, where the legendary New York deejay Frankie "Hollywood" Crocker threw parties for a surprisingly integrated crowd. But before all these incarnations, this basement was the crown jewel of Manhattan nightclubs—Birdland.

Named after bebop pioneer and free spirit Charlie "Bird" Parker and owned by reputed ▶ PG 65

Dinah Washington

Dinah Washington could really apply a blues interpretation to a pop song: she just knew how to bend all the notes and take it away from the melody just enough so that she put her trademark on it. Nobody would sing a version like that but her.

I met her at the Apollo Theatre, and she became a great friend to me. I used to write arrangements for her band on the road, and eventually she just insisted that I write the arrangements for her records.

I always saw a sweet side of her, a vulnerable side. But I've seen her take an ex-husband's clothes that she'd bought and put all of the clothes and shoes and hats and overcoats in the bathtub and pour kerosene on it and set it on fire. You know—"It's all over!"

She lived like her songs were—I've seen her in the middle of a show, in public, almost dismissing one of her boyfriends, or husbands, on the stand. Like: "Ladies and gentlemen, you're looking at the last night this man will be up here on the stage." She could really bust them. She was something. –Q

At the end of the concert in *Cyprus,* all of these

same students that stoned the embassy rushed the stage

and they grabbed *Dizzy.* We thought we were all

in trouble. And they put him on their shoulders and

they were cheering him! –Quincy

Adam Clayton Powell called me to Washington and said,

"I'm going to propose to Congress that we send a big

band overseas to the **Near East,** *the* **Middle East,**

and **South America."** *So I got in touch with Quincy.*

He took care of organizing the band, the arrangements.

All I had to do was play. –*Dizzy Gillespie*

The weapon

that we will use is

THE COOL ONE.

–Dizzy Gillespie

mobster and authentic music mogul Morris Levy, Birdland was famous the world over as a showcase for bands and players on the cutting edge of modern jazz. Down the street from Roseland and a few blocks from the clubs jammed together along 52nd Street, Birdland was a magnet for young ambitious players like Quincy, drawing them from the hinterlands to the city that jazz musicians had labeled the Big Apple.

The city itself was many things to the young and eager—emporium, playground, training and testing center, a place where geniuses resided and the mantle of greatness could be bestowed. They had no time for white big-band music—bebop, also called modern, was the harmonically complex sound of the elite players and their sophisticated audiences.

The name came from an underground language called jive that passed from hipster to hip-

ster, player to player. At after-hours clubs like Minton's Playhouse in Harlem, a loose grouping of musical nonconformists such as trumpeter Dizzy Gillespie, saxophonist Charlie "Bird" Parker, drummer Kenny Clarke, and pianists Thelonious Monk and Bud Powell were exploring a "modern" approach to jazz, one that liberated gifted players from the strictures of dance music by emphasizing the virtuosity of the solo instrument instead of a danceable beat. Experimenting, competing, challenging and provoking one another to new sounds, the musicians stretched the rhythmic and harmonic limits of improvised music. Rhythms came so fast that unsteady players were swept off the bandstand. The beboppers played old standards, but for their chords, not their melodies, using them as bases for long solo improvisations. Many who loved swing hated bebop, and even audiences that respected the ambition of the musicians found the actual music difficult to follow —where was the melody? But while the traditionalists balked, youngbloods found in bebop the challenge to their hearts, their ears, and their techniques. Bebop demanded much more than mere competence on a given instrument, and Quincy struggled to match the music's exacting standards with his solo skills.

There wasn't a lot of money to be made in bebop, but then, money wasn't what bebop was about. With the naive optimism characteristic of the decade after the war, and with a dedication to art for art's sake rare in the American experience, this largely African-American community spun out blatantly self-referential, intensely personal music in nightclubs all around midtown Manhattan.

Quincy got his first taste of the Big Apple in 1951, when he took the train down from Boston to arrange music for a recording session for a friend from Seattle, bass-playing bandleader Oscar Pettiford. Quincy was paid a whopping $17 a song, but there were compen-

DIZZY GILLESPIE WITH DON BYAS, PARIS, 1952

Jazz was forbidden during the war. So right after the liberation of France, this music exploded all over, **because it was friendly** —we could drink and eat to this music. – Michel LeGrand

France evokes many of the warmest, most vivid *memories of* my entire life. In a way, *Europe* helped me to define myself as a young musician, and my place in the world. –Quincy

His heart was always there and I know that now.

sations more important than money. After the session was done, Quincy and Pettiford hit the streets. "We went to Birdland and a place called Snookie's, and we went to the Blue Note; 52nd Street was jumping then. And somehow that part of New York was bright and beautiful. It looked gorgeous ... You'd go down the street, and man, there was Basie's band and Sarah Vaughan and Billy Eckstine and Redd Foxx. Duke was there, too. It was ridiculous, it was so hot."

Then Quincy met Charlie Parker. "We went to Big Nick's on 110th," Quincy remembers, "and Bird said, 'Let's buy some weed.' And I said, 'That's hip.' When you're eighteen years old, you want to be down with the dudes. So we go to some place on, I think, 139th Street. Bird was sweating a lot—had a white shirt on and a big belly. One button was off and I could see some of his meat. So we go to this place and I felt like one of the dudes. I was with Bird. I had about twenty dollars left from the two arrangements and Bird said, 'Let me hold the money.' It started raining and we were out in front of this raggedy place on 139th. Bird said, 'You stay right here. We'll be right back.' After forty minutes I was starting to get the message. Then I started to cry." Bird had dogged Quincy, and the teenager had to walk all the way back to midtown. Still the incident only strengthened his resolve to stop being a musical tourist and become one of the cats on the inside.

Bebop wasn't just a sound, it was an attitude toward living that spilled over the bandstand edge. Beboppers sported sharp-as-tacks vives (aka clothes), and ultrahip dudes like Dizzy set off whole fashion trends by sporting berets and growing goatees. They used narcotics liberally, primarily marijuana or "reefer," but also, with tragic results, heroin; in some ways, the self-consciously "hip" scene prefigured the drug culture of the 1960s. A number of black musicians had romances with white women, sometimes more to express individual freedom and ▶ PG 72

QUINCY AND JOLIE

He came once, when I was in junior high, to spend some time at the school. I guess he had an arrangement that wasn't done. He was in the back of my classroom writing an arrangement. You know, you kind of just wished that Dad would just come and watch your stuff.

—Jolie Jones Levine

Nadia Boulanger's spirit is so strongly in me, it's unbelievable. Because a lot of the things that she used to talk to me about as a student I mentally was not prepared to accept. She used to intimidate a lot of classical students, because that was the mecca for them, but if you're talking about a bebopper that's been drinking wine since he was fourteen, it was another kind of a thing.

She told me about principles that I wasn't willing to accept yet, about freedom in music. That you have no freedom until you establish boundaries and parameters. She was absolutely right. She said, "If you have all the freedom you want when you're going to write a piece of music, you end up writing nothing, because, at one time or another, you have to say, 'I'm gonna use eighteen instruments, and I'm gonna have two minutes of this being slow, and then it'll go to three minutes of fast, and it'll be loud, or soft,' or whatever."

She was absolutely right, those are the decisions that you're always making. And she always talked about the power of melody, that melody was king. Melody was king. She just drove that into your head.

And she said to me, "Forget about the great American symphony. The untapped music roots of your own music need to be dealt with." And she put me on that path. –Q

If I said to Quincy, "I think the second eight mea-sures don't seem to fit with the *mood* of the rest of the thing — he'd go ten feet away and *fix it.* It always *amazed* me that a man could do that — to change all of these notes that he had written before. –Frank Sinatra

See, some guys write the same way for every-body: his arrangements **accompanied** *the singer.* –Billy Eckstine

The best results I've had,

as it happened,

were when we

surrendered

to each other. —Quincy

radicalism than real love. The prevailing feeling was contempt for the hypocrisies of "square" society or for conventional cultural forms. The American government, beboppers said, didn't abide by the Bill of Rights in its treatment of "Negroes," so why should they honor its rules of behavior in their everyday lives? Their contempt underlay the attitude of "cool," an aesthetic of emotional distance that allowed those in and around the music to keep an often hostile world at arm's length, and to go after their own new definition of greatness.

And the world was, indeed, hostile to bebop, or at least resistant to this intentionally non-melodic, improvisational style that was nearly impossible to dance to. Quincy says, "Miles [Davis], Dizzy, Ray Brown, Charlie Parker, Thelonious Monk, Charlie Mingus, all the bebop dudes—they were the generation of jazz musicians, and they thought it was unhip to be too successful. They said, 'We don't want to be entertainers. We want to be artists. We want to explore.' And when they went into bebop, we lost some of our greatest warriors, because the public rejected them and they didn't make a dime, not a dime. I mean, they lived from day to day. And they went into this little cocoon and we ended up with a lot of casualties—a lot of people in the gutter, dying from heroin."

Quincy desperately wanted to join the New York scene, but he needed a job and a salary and he wasn't going to find them in a bebop club. When the opportunity to join Lionel Hampton's band presented itself in 1951, Quincy left Berklee and Boston. It might seem strange that a bebop fanatic would join an organization at the opposite end of the performing spectrum, but Hampton's decidedly traditional big-band style had a verve that caught the fancy of the musician in Quincy. Hampton was a total entertainer; his attitude was the antithesis of art for art's sake. His performing values had been molded by the period when swing was dominant and enjoyed

QUINCY AND SARAH VAUGHAN, PARIS

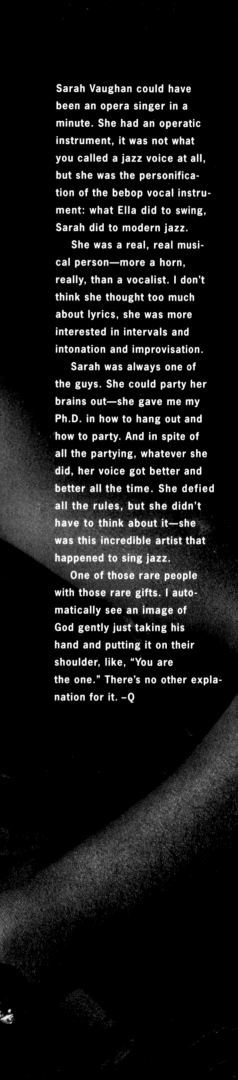

Sarah Vaughan could have been an opera singer in a minute. She had an operatic instrument, it was not what you called a jazz voice at all, but she was the personification of the bebop vocal instrument: what Ella did to swing, Sarah did to modern jazz.

She was a real, real musical person—more a horn, really, than a vocalist. I don't think she thought too much about lyrics, she was more interested in intervals and intonation and improvisation.

Sarah was always one of the guys. She could party her brains out—she gave me my Ph.D. in how to hang out and how to party. And in spite of all the partying, whatever she did, her voice got better and better all the time. She defied all the rules, but she didn't have to think about it—she was this incredible artist that happened to sing jazz.

One of those rare people with those rare gifts. I automatically see an image of God gently just taking his hand and putting it on their shoulder, like, "You are the one." There's no other explanation for it. –Q

Sarah Vaughan

by both races, and rollicking tent shows brought live entertainment to blacks across the rural South. From his fancy vibraphone riffs to his toothy smile, Hampton's efforts were directed entirely at getting the crowd cheering and jiving. His band's style harked back to the crazed showmanship of Cab Calloway's outfits in the thirties and prefigured the touring R&B revues to come in the fifties and sixties. A seasoned pro, Hampton had an enormous amount to teach a neophyte trumpeter about the touring business, and Quincy's arrangements gave a lot back to the band. "Lionel Hampton was a superstar back then," says Quincy. "He had the first rock'n'roll band in America. I'm talking about that big beat sound with the honking tenor sax and the screaming high note trumpet. Hamp was a showman. He had us wearing these outlandish purple outfits—matching coats and shorts and socks and Tyrolean hats." A typical evening's appearance opened with a tap dancer, a vocal quartet, a male and female singer, and a comic before Hampton himself began his set.

Hampton's band featured several brilliant young players, including trumpeters Art Farmer and Quincy's close friend Clifford Brown. "Brownie really touched my soul every night," Quincy recalls. "He was an astounding musician; he had it all—the science, the technique, the soul, the imagination, the freshness. I haven't heard him beaten yet. Clifford's aura is still something I feel." Night after night Hamp's band played swing in every theater and ballroom in every city, every state; but in the back of the tour bus, in segregated "black only" hotels, at Harlem nightspots, and on those rare occasions when he got back to his Third Avenue apartment, the nineteen-year-old trumpeter-arranger continued to study bebop in New York's cool community.

Quincy worked on and off with Hampton from 1951 to 1959, an era with a reputation today for being relatively uninspiring musically. True, the biggest popular hits were, by and large,

the same old stuff, but beneath that placid surface, a lot of new ideas were coming to a boil. Bebop continued to evolve, and jazz and blues singers were beginning to record without big-band backing or orchestrations, picking up on some of the solo innovations of the "moderns." Rhythm and blues and its adolescent cousin, rock'n'roll, were starting to flourish. Even middlebrow audiences at Broadway theaters were finding themselves startled by new musical productions that moved far from the comic operettas of old. Music and musicians were on the move all over and Quincy began to widen his range to incorporate as much of the new musical information as he could.

Throughout his life, Quincy has been open to new technology, experimenting in areas where many of his otherwise radical bebop peers grew conservative. Quincy never let his passion for pure bebop limit his interest in other ways to make sounds, and in 1953, he took a brave step by arranging an Art Farmer album to feature Monk Montgomery on an early prototype for the electric bass. "The electric bass and the electric guitar, which came out in 1939, revolutionized music and laid the foundation of rock'n' roll," he explains. "The [electric] bass's sound was so imposing compared to the upright bass, and it couldn't have the same function. You couldn't just have it playing 4/4 lines—it had too much personality. Before the electric bass and guitar, the rhythm section was the support section, backing up the horns and piano. But when they were introduced, everything upstairs had to take the back seat. The rhythm section became the stars … It created a new language, showing the relationship between technology and aesthetics." Jazz was fueled by interest in rhythmic dance music and in the new R&B riffs. Quincy had the musical insight to assemble these combinations of elements —and it resulted not only in albums like Farmer's; one day he'd use the same combinations to produce the global phenomenon Michael Jackson. ▶ PG 78

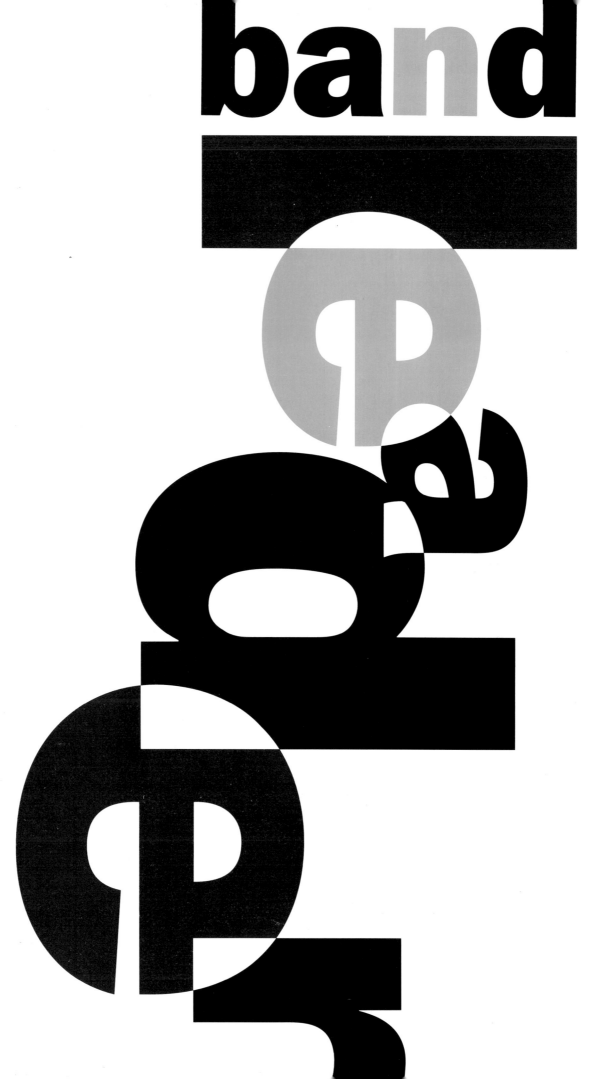

Later in 1953, Quincy went with Hampton's band to Europe, where, in contrast to America, audiences appreciated and enthusiastically supported jazz efforts. He led a group of moonlighting band members in a series of recording sessions, and these releases—which included *Quincy Jones and the Swedish All-Stars* and *Stockholm Sweetnin'*—established Quincy as a special hero to fanatical European jazz buffs.

The next year Quincy was out of Hampton's band and back in New York. Launching himself as a jack-of-all-arrangements, he might in the course of one week write charts for Hampton to take out on the road; guide ballplayer-turned-crooner Willie Mays through his vocal debut on "Say Hey Willie Mays," with the flamboyant R&B vocal group the Treniers; and work on recording sessions with Dizzy Gillespie, pianist George Wallington, and singer Helen Merrill. During 1954, Quincy also met two women des-

The calmness and

professionalism

that he possessed,

just standing there.

Looking at this kid,

you know. He had all

this in those days.

—Clark Terry

It was a big, **BIG FAMILY.** The whole

tined to figure prominently in his musical life: the "Queen of the Blues," Dinah Washington, and her four-year-old goddaughter, Patti Austin. Washington, a true diva with a passionate singing style and a temper to match, was the dominant African-American female vocalist of the age. She and Quincy developed a strong friendship, and she fought to have him (and other black musicians) work on her recordings whenever possible.

While working on a session with her in Chicago, Quincy began a friendship that years later would blossom into a fruitful collaboration. Bruce Swedien was an engineer at Universal recording studios in Chicago who, says Quincy, "had a similar background to mine. He'd done all the great jazz greats, funk bands, Natalie Cole, at Chess with Willie Dixon. Bruce was the engineer on Gene Chandler's 'Duke of Earl,' and he did Chuck Berry. He was also with the Chicago Symphony for eleven years!" Swedien and Quincy did session work together, and would match their talents on projects all the way through to Michael Jackson's *Bad* and Quincy's own *Back on the Block*.

Swedien's talents would also prove useful to Quincy when he went to Hollywood. ▶ PG 83

BIG BAND thing was about a family. –Quincy

A lot of these jazz purist "critics" would rather

a jazz musician, when he dies,

be found in an old rat-infested hotel with a bottle of

BOOZE in his hand and a **NEEDLE** in his

arm. And they say, "Oh, he died, he's

an **IMMORTAL."**

The hell with that. –Billy Eckstine

I met Billy Eckstine when I was fifteen years old. He was the most beautiful-looking man you ever saw in your life—he wasn't good looking, he was pretty.

Billy had a sound that was not stereotypical of a black singer at that time. He had almost a classical voice, which people hadn't heard before—for somebody to have a voice that was almost an operatic baritone and sing jazz and beautiful love ballads. It just threw everybody off. And to have a black sex symbol then was unheard of.

But Eckstine's essence was about class, basically, it was about pride. He didn't sing dumb "oogum boogum" songs, he sang pretty melodies that had meaningful words. There was an incredible element of class and taste involved at all times—the way he dressed, the way he spoke, the way he presented his music. And he was very hip and stylish—when I was a kid, you were really a nerd if you didn't have Mr. B collars on.

You could see how he would front the band that would be the revolutionary bebop band. The spawning ground, with Dexter Gordon and Gene Ammons and Leo Parker and Charlie Parker and J.J. Johnson and Art Blakey and Miles and Dizzy and Sarah Vaughan on piano. That was the birth of the cool, that was the birth of the whole revolution. –Q

B

illy Eckstine

Quincy picked the *cream* of young

QUINCY JONES ORCHESTRA, PARIS FREE AND EASY TOUR

musicians. —Dizzy Gillespie

"Bruce is the only engineer I know who can do the prerecording on a film, the location shooting, the post-scoring, the dubbing, and the album as well. It's knowing 360 degrees of your stuff."

1955: Benny Carter, Cannonball Adderley

Quincy spent 1955 shuttling between a basement apartment on West 95th Street and various recording studios where he supervised an eclectic string of records, including work by gospel pioneer James Cleveland, Benny Carter, Mouseketeer Darlene Gillespie, Jon Hendricks of the jazz vocal trio Lambert, Hendricks & Ross, blues belter Big Maybelle, and Dinah Washington. His reputation was snowballing with each gig, and he found himself spending as much time writing charts for singers as he did for bands. Working with two new young talents provided the year's highlights: he discovered saxophonist Julian "Cannonball" Adderley and recorded his first solo album. Later in the year, while arranging the scores for Tommy Dorsey's summer replacement show on CBS (his first television gig), he met a young sensation named Elvis Presley. Dorsey, an unreconstructed big-band star, hated Elvis, but Quincy was impressed by his intense showmanship.

1956: The State Department Tour, First Album

In 1956, Quincy was about to start working at Columbia with Johnny Mathis, a twenty-year-old track star with an angelic voice, when Dizzy Gillespie called. The State Department, suddenly aware of bebop's popularity abroad, had invited Dizzy to tour the Middle East and South America as part of a goodwill campaign designed to overcome the "Ugly American" image. Remembering his earlier happy times in Europe and eager to escape the everyday drudgery of session work, Quincy signed on as organizer. In Rio he began lifelong friendships with samba innovators Antonio Carlos Jobim, João and Astrude ▶ PG 86

WHEN HE HAD THE CHANCE TO BE MUSIC DIRECTOR FOR HAROLD ARLEN'S SHOW, *Free and Easy,*

HE ASKED ME TO BE HIS ASSISTANT. I SAID, fantastic!

WE PUT THE BAND TOGETHER. HE HAD A FANTASTIC BAND.

QUINCY JUST CARRIED US ALL OVER EUROPE.

We were a family —Clark Terry

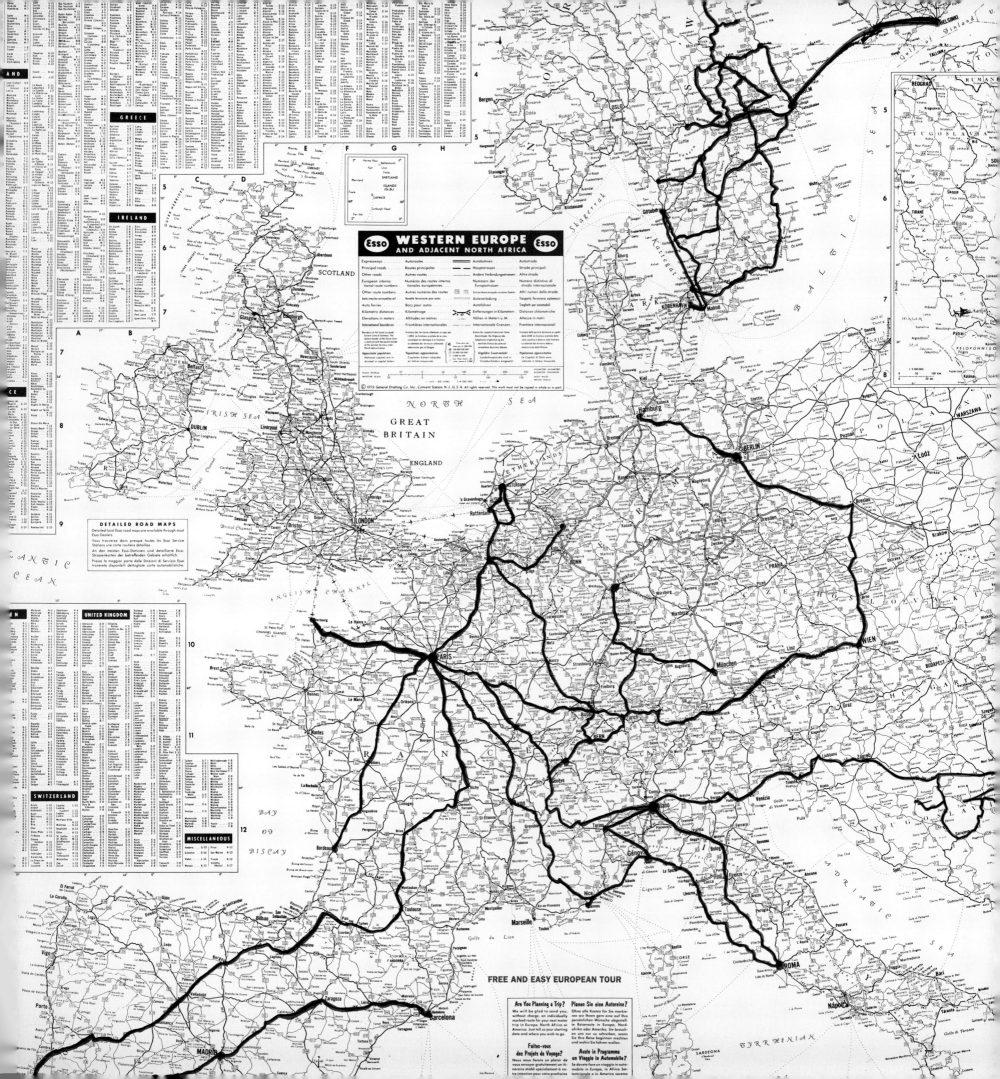

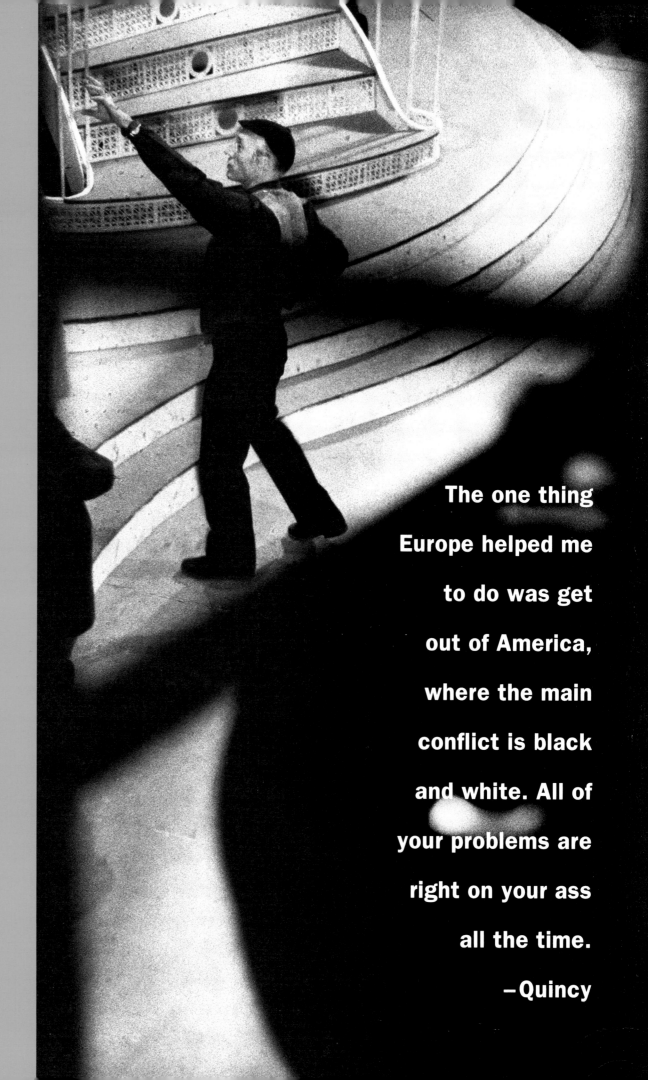

Gilberto, and other leaders in the Brazilian club scene. He was taking a long, delightful taste of international jazz stardom, and loving it.

Back at home in September of the same year, Quincy took a major artistic step; he cut his first album as bandleader. *This Is How I Feel about Jazz* was recorded in New York with an all-star crew of musicians: Charlie Mingus and Paul Chambers on bass, Hank Jones and Billy Taylor on piano, Phil Woods on saxophone, Art Farmer on trumpet. In his liner notes, Quincy wrote, "I would prefer not to have this music categorized at all, for it's probably influenced by every original voice in and outside jazz, maybe anyone from blues singer Ray Charles to Ravel."

1957: Barclay Disque, Nadia Boulanger

The year 1957 began back in New York, where the buzz of playing bebop on the road had given way once more to the creative tedium of session work. But the daily grind wasn't the worst part of the job; much more discouraging was the racism that faced Quincy in the studio. Talent, the studio executives apparently felt, had a racial component. Black arrangers were allowed to supervise the rhythm section and the horns, but weren't considered skilled enough to handle strings. This was a long-standing convention in popular music. Strings were regarded as sophisticated instruments, and it was looked upon as a radical move to allow even Billie Holiday to use them as accompaniment; they were for the likes of Sinatra or Tony Bennett. During the fifties, race prejudices against performers were slowly fading but had not yet diminished for black arrangers, who were thought to lack "subtlety." Quincy felt the bias was a clear slap in the face to him as an artist, and it also cut him out of significant income, as all too often a second arranger would be brought in to complete the orchestral sequences.

Out of the blue came the break—from ▶ **PG 96**

> **The one thing Europe helped me to do was get out of America, where the main conflict is black and white. All of your problems are right on your ass all the time.**
> **–Quincy**

You don't have to watch your back in France.
Even now, you know, when a black person walks in a club,
the first thing they do is find out how to get out of it. —Miles Davis

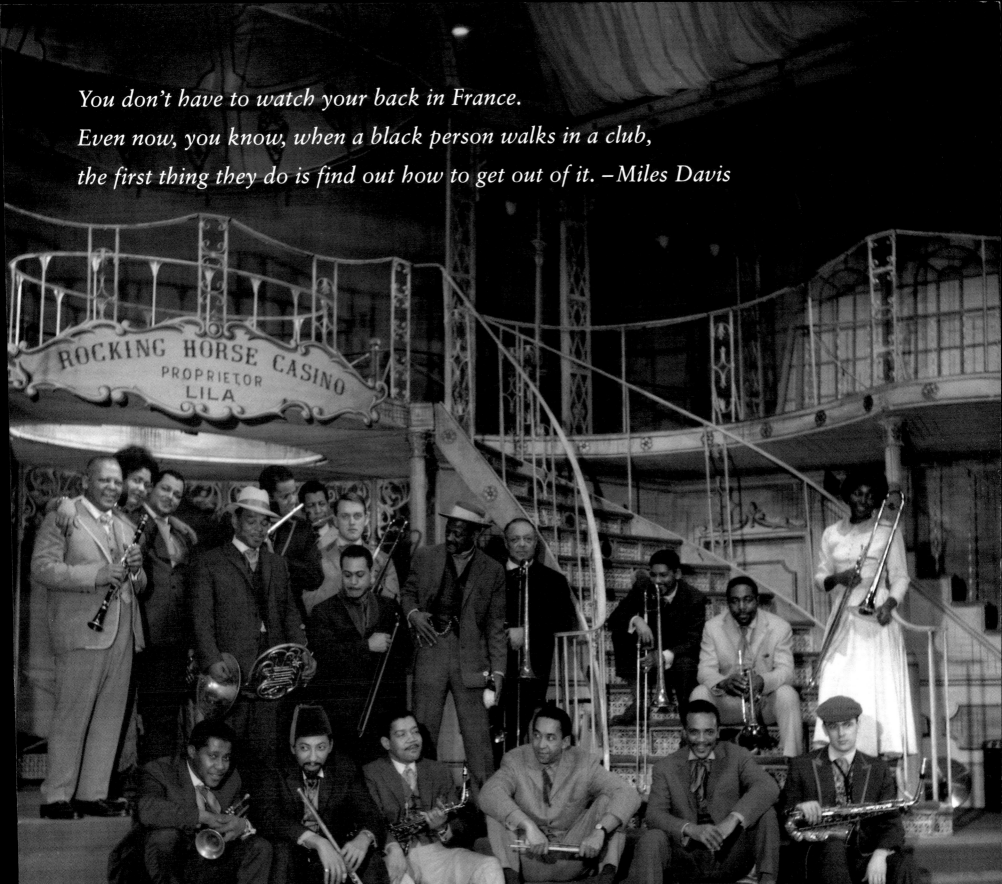

I had **LUDICROUS** optimism.

"We're totally

gonna

make

it, man.

This is *gonna work,* you know?

We got a great band and *it's gonna work.*" –Quincy

I had no management, agents, nothing.

I didn't realize what the business side was about

...and I had a payroll that I had to come up with every week,

no matter what happened. —Quincy

There were money problems

and then they were stuck over there. —Jolie Jones Levine

I couldn't handle it.

I couldn't go on.

It was a nightmare, a nightmare.

Just to survive from day to day. —Quincy

He did everything he could to try and make the band work.

The tour was a bust. —Irv Green

That's the closest I ever came in my life to suicide. —Quincy

I think there were many thoughts in his mind

that this was the end of the world for him. —Irv Green

I had a responsibility to get them home

even if it meant that I'd be in debt for seven years. —Quincy

&man

I was behind that desk every day... **Awful!**

You had to be in there at **nine o'clock,** and you

He came back and went to work in our New York office. —Irv Green

had to wear these **Italian suits.** You had to fill

It was a day job. He actually had to go to work. —Jolie Jones Levine

out **expense reports** and all that kind of stuff

That really *made my skin crawl.* —Quincy

JACK TRACY, IRVIN GREEN, QUINCY, CLYDE OTIS, PARIS 1958

We had this record...this girl was sixteen years old...and every-body turned it down after listening to it. But Quincy...

I said, "Well, pop music is not that big a deal to do." So that record, I took as a ...as a kind of a challenge, and said, "Okay."

GUYS WERE ALWAYS TEASING ME AND HAL MOONEY THAT WE WERE BUDGET BUSTERS,

BECAUSE WE JUST RECORDED GOOD MUSIC THAT NEVER MADE MONEY...

–QUINCY

Europe. Quincy was asked to become musical director for Eddie Barclay's label, in Paris. That Barclay Disque, a European company, would place an African-American in charge of its musical operations, putting its financial fate squarely in his hands, revealed the distance America still had to travel to match the social attitudes in Europe, at least in the musical world, and it also highlighted how immense Quincy's reputation was on the Continent. His new life in Paris gave him amazing new creative opportunities, and he won awards in Sweden, Germany, and France for his conducting and arranging. Black expatriate writers James Baldwin and Richard Wright, singer Josephine Baker, and Pablo Picasso were among his friends. Ever the student, he spent many evenings studying with legendary French instructor Nadia Boulanger. Many years later, Mme. Boulanger said that her two most distinguished students had been Igor Stravinsky and Quincy Jones.

Quincy's new address didn't cause him to neglect his American connections, however, and he continued to handle sessions featuring Americans abroad, including *Vaughan and Violins*, for Sarah Vaughan, and Basie's *One More Time*. Supported by the Barclay orchestra, he charted a special performance by Frank Sinatra for Princess Grace of Monaco.

1959: Count Basie, Birth of the Band, Free and Easy European Tour

One of the most turbulent years in his life, 1959, began auspiciously. A new release shattered any doubts that Quincy could be as forceful a bandleader as he was an arranger. Recorded in New York, *Birth of a Band* featured his old mentor Clark Terry and Hampton alumni Art Farmer and Jimmy Cleveland, and included a tribute to Clifford Brown, who'd died in an auto accident the year before. Other important recordings that year included *Count Basie with Strings*, a session with Basie and Billy Eckstine, and *The Genius of*

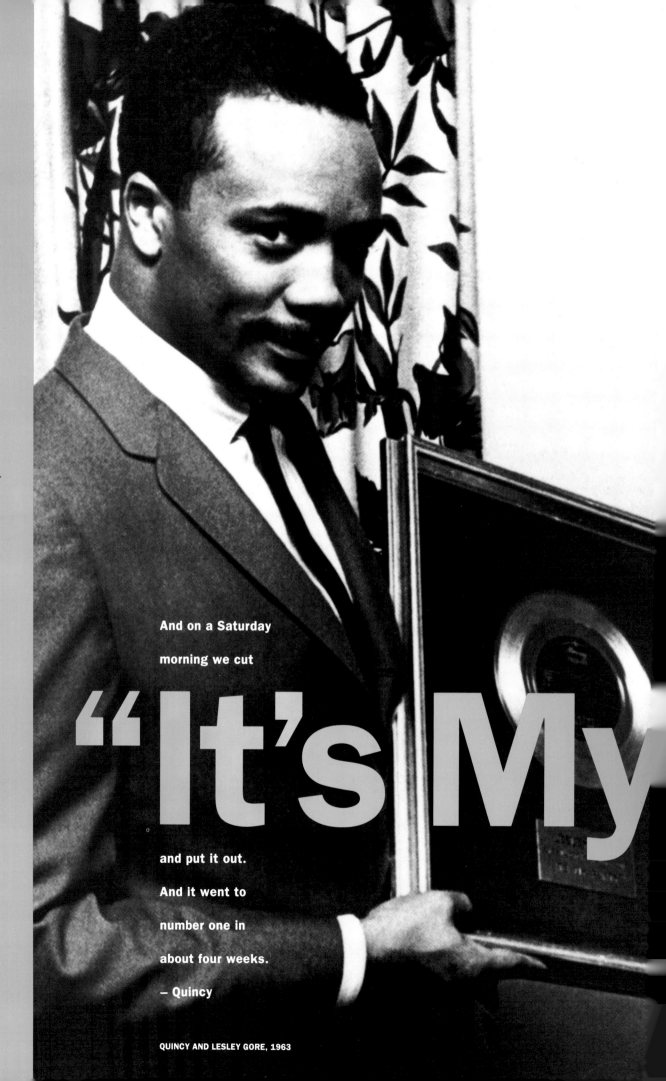

And on a Saturday morning we cut

"It's My

and put it out. And it went to number one in about four weeks.

— Quincy

QUINCY AND LESLEY GORE, 1963

Party"

Certain paperboys can go in any yard

with any dogs and they won't get bit.

He just has it. —Miles Davis

Ray Charles, an album on which the old friends skillfully blended Charles's soul singing style with ambitious big-band jazz charts.

Later in the year, Quincy organized an all-star band to tour Europe with a revival of the Johnny Mercer–Harold Arlen musical *Free and Easy*. The show was supposed to play throughout Europe before moving to London, where Sammy Davis, Jr., was to join the cast; and the goal was Broadway. The production folded in Paris, but Quincy was in love with the sound of the ensemble and decided to keep the band together. Musically, it was a marvelous platform for Quincy, and he was banking on his European reputation to find enough work to meet the weekly payroll. But he had miscalculated badly and soon found himself scrambling to find gigs for the group. At one point he booked his musicians on a slow train from Spain to Yugoslavia, flew to Paris to supervise an Andy Williams date, and then grabbed a flight to Yugoslavia, just to have some cash on hand when the band arrived.

By borrowing money and selling off his publishing catalogue, practically giving away the rights to every composition he'd written at that point, Quincy raised enough money to send the band home. Quincy has often said that that star-crossed tour was so devastating that it made him consider suicide. It was a humbling experience that left him in debt and illustrated how much he had to learn about the business of music. At this low point in Quincy's life, the chief of Mercury Records, Irvin Green, entered the scene.

1961: First Black Vice President of a Major Record Company

The business side of popular commercial music in 1961 was dominated by whites. Black artists might star in the relatively small realms of jazz and R&B; Fats Domino and Chuck Berry had their following, and an artist like Nat King Cole might win the mainstream audience over, but this

lla Fitzgerald

If Sarah Vaughan is the trumpet player, then Ella is the driving tenor player. She's the tenor player that drives it—never lets the phrase stay behind, she's constantly searching for it, because she's got a forward motion that just never stops. She's a swing machine.

Like Sarah, she considers herself an instrumentalist first. But Ella's so humble, she doesn't think she can sing. She really doesn't.

Ella's very hip, too—everything that comes out, she's right on top of it, she even said she wanted to write some rap tunes. She knows what's going on, she pays attention. I guess even back then, too, they considered it to be hip to be on top of everything, and to this day she's still there. I remember talking to Ella on the phone one day, and she started singing the theme to *Sanford and Son* to me. I couldn't believe it.

I put Sarah and Ella on the same song on *Back on the Block* because I'd never heard of them ever being on the same record before, and they are my favorites. They give me goose bumps. They didn't know at the time, though, that they were on the same song. And I thought that was just fine that way. Two of the best that ever did it. –Q

YOU HAVE TO *feel the pulse* OF WHAT'S

HAPPENING AROUND YOU, THEN PUT YOUR OWN SEAL ON IT. YOU STAY CURRENT, YOU

STAY MODERN, YOU **stay up to date.**

BUT YOU WEAR THE CLOTHES THAT FIT YOU. —RAY CHARLES

FROM THE DAY I MET QUINCY, I KNEW THAT YOU COULD PUT ANYTHING IN

HIS HANDS AND IT WOULD COME OUT THE WAY YOU WANTED IT TO COME OUT. —IRV GREEN

EVERY ONE OF US IN THIS BUSINESS WANTS TO BE A LITTLE MORE. *That's the only way you learn.* I MEAN, MY GOSH, I THINK THE NEXT THING

I'M GONNA TRY IS RAP! —ELLA FITZGERALD

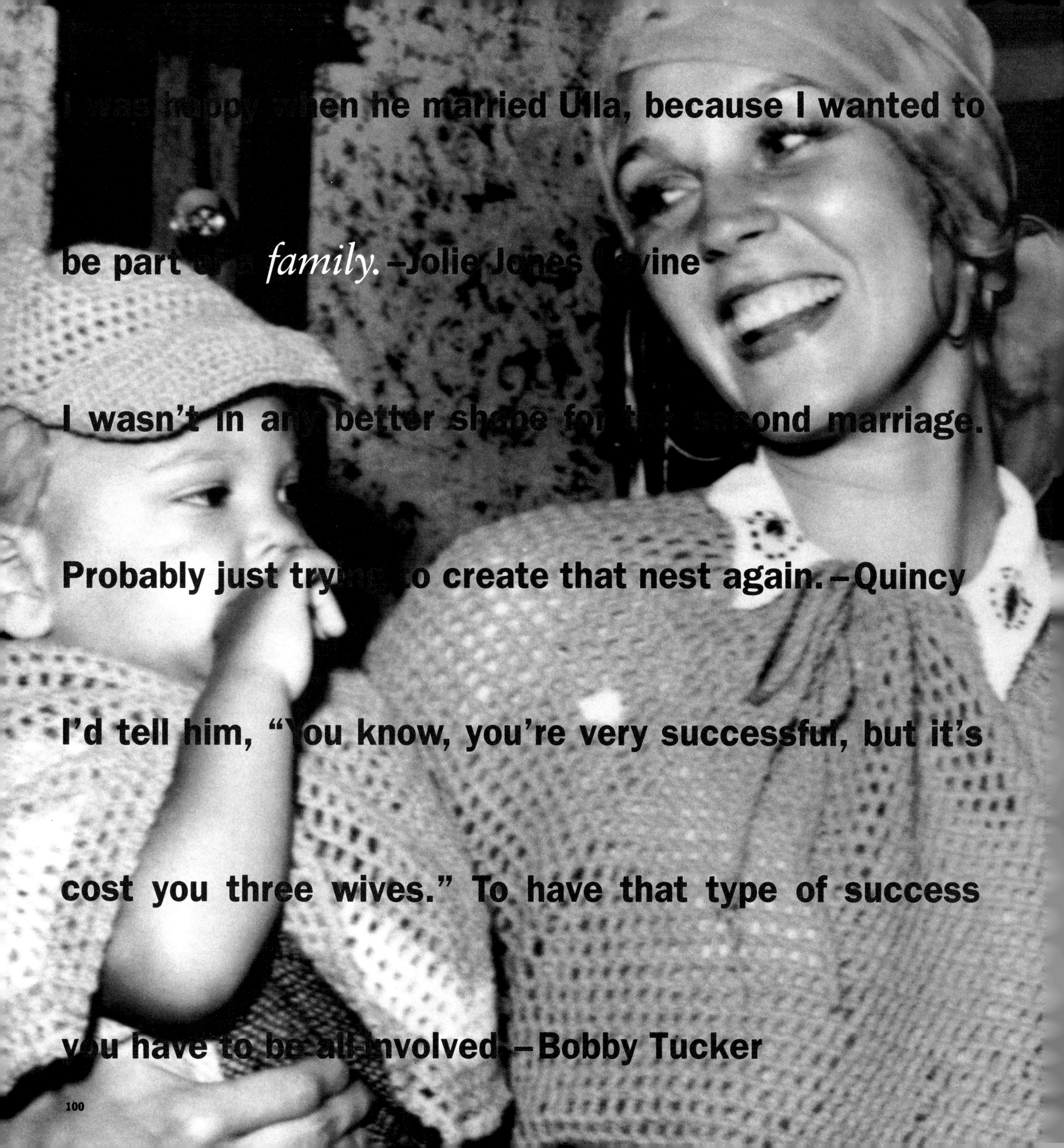

I was happy when he married Ulla, because I wanted to

be part of a *family.* —Jolie Jones Levine

I wasn't in any better shape for the second marriage.

Probably just trying to create that nest again. —Quincy

I'd tell him, "You know, you're very successful, but it's

cost you three wives." To have that type of success

you have to be all involved. —Bobby Tucker

was the era before the rise of Motown or the explosion of soul over the AM airwaves. Black entrepreneurs were almost unknown on any mass scale, and the idea of a black executive for a major label was nearly unthinkable. It was a daring move indeed for Irvin Green to ask Quincy Jones to join Mercury in talent development, and in 1962 to promote him to become the first black vice president in the business.

Green explains, "I saw things in Quincy that I thought were very business-oriented. He was quite a businessman, and had a great personality —knew how to negotiate, even contracts." In the established record world, Mercury was, admittedly, something of a rebel label; it's unlikely that anyone at Decca, Columbia, or RCA would have dreamed of hiring a black man, even one of Quincy Jones's talent, for an executive position.

Quincy worked hard in his new position— in 1963 alone, he logged almost 250,000 miles in visits to Holland, Italy, Great Britain, and Japan, representing Mercury's interests—and it was quickly clear that Green's faith in him was not misplaced. Quincy won his first Grammy as a jazz arranger in 1962 for interpreting Ray Charles's "I Can't Stop Loving You" for Count Basie. He performed with Billy Eckstine and at benefits, and put his magical touch to new records by Ella Fitzgerald, Sarah Vaughan, saxophonist Roland Kirk, and an instrumental version of the score for *Golden Boy*.

1963: Lesley Gore, Frank Sinatra

By 1963, bebop's innovative energy had dissipated. Performers on the leading edge of improvisational music still tapped into bop ideas, but John Coltrane, Miles Davis, and Ornette Coleman were putting their own idiosyncratic spin on that tradition. The Fender electric bass, a curiosity when Quincy originally worked with it, was now an industry staple. Its vibrant personality and flexibility on vinyl, alongside the ▶ PG 110

QUINCY III, ULLA AND QUINCY

My baby, my uncle, my mentor, my father, my brother, my friend, was Count Basie.
I met Basie when I was thirteen years old at the Palomar Theater in Seattle,
and our friendship lasted the rest of his life. –Quincy

One time up in Hartford, Connect-icut, we played the Elks Club ball and only about seven or eight hundred people showed up. And I was really depressed, because we had this big band and there was supposed to be about three thousand people. The promoter paid me, and Basie said, "Well, what did you do with the money?" I said, "I kept it to pay my bank." He said, "Give him half of the money back." I said, "What do you mean?"

He said, "He put your name out front, and the people didn't show up. You shouldn't punish him, because he may be the man in two or three years from now that's gonna have to help you get another job."

That's why he stayed in busi-ness fifty or sixty years. Because he just was a very fair, ethical man with a lot of integrity. Basie was just really regular folks, very, very down to earth. Basie was very real. –Q

ount Basie

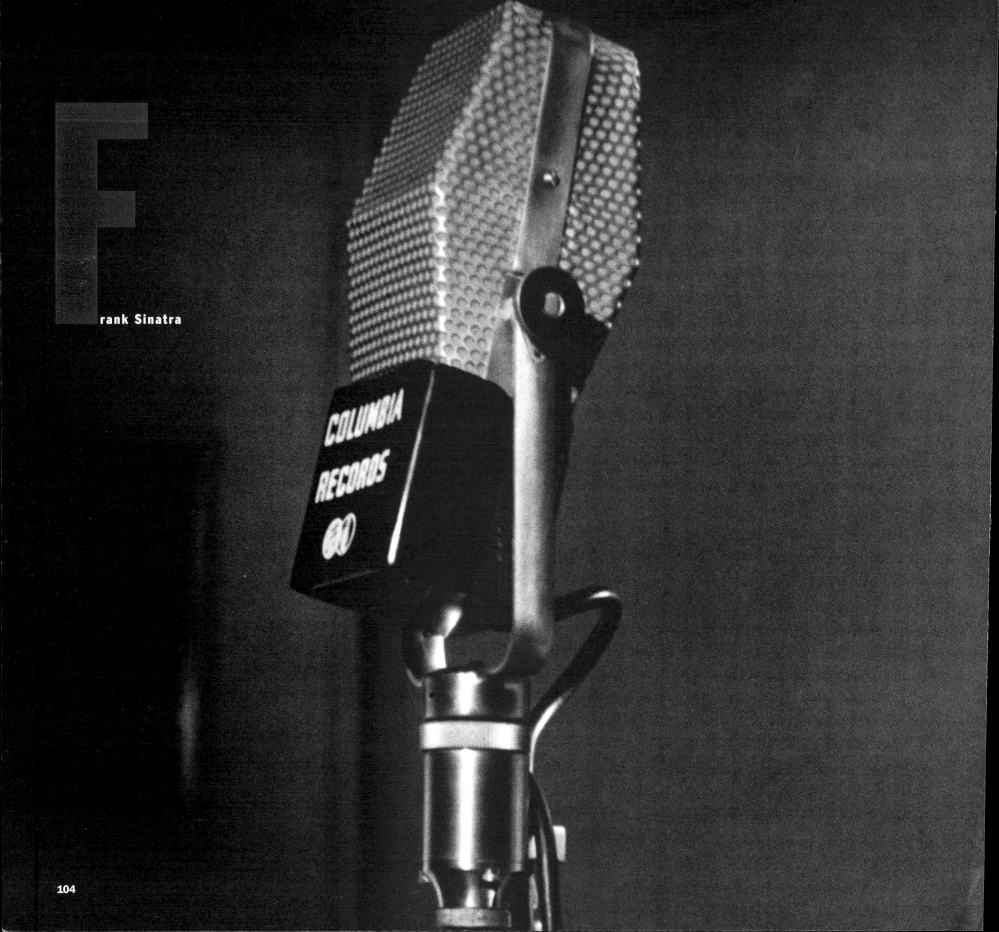

Frank Sinatra

Frank Sinatra has always astounded me, because he's just such a great singer, with musicality and daring. He's really a daring singer—he takes an instrumental approach to singing, the way he phrases on top of the rhythm section. It's very important how a singer sings on top of the rhythm section. Some sing straight up and down, or lag a lot, but Frank puts it right in the pocket. And he has more respect for arrangers than any living singer I've ever seen.

The electricity of 1965, when Frank was really in his peak singing form and we did the Sands in Las Vegas with the Basie Band...I've never been so excited about going to work every night. And neither were "Frank and Splank."

Frank almost jumped off the stage some nights. He'd say, "Goddamn!" He just couldn't believe it. Because everything felt so good: Basie's band was so mellow—they had the ability to just stay down there and simmer, keep everything on fire playing very softly—it was like flames on the stand, when we'd go out there. I'll never forget it. –Q

If Ray had followed the strict commercial line, he may have had more hits, but he would have had less meaning. People buy an armful of Ray Charles cassettes or discs, and what they're buying is an armful of **integrity.** –Jesse Jackson

"Every music has its soul. And if you really are sincere and surrender to it and explore it, it's all soulful." –Ray Charles

*When he became the vice president in charge of **A**rtists & **R**epertoire of Mercury Records, the first black person to reach that level, I absolutely was so proud,*  *it was just unbelievable. And then he says, "I'm going out to Hollywood!!"* –Lloyd Jones

I just dropped everything and just took that chance. I said, "Maybe I won't make it out there, but **I'm going!**" –Quincy

electric guitar, trap drums, and increasingly sophisticated recording equipment, were in the process of permanently altering the way music was physically produced and the way we heard it.

These new aural possibilities were also changing roles in the studio. The arranger, once the chief supervisor in any session, was being supplanted by the producer. The key to a successful record was no longer just directing the sound of the band, but controlling the technical aspects of assembling the record itself. Multi-tracking studios and overdubbing made it possible to create dense layers of sound built not by musicians but by the engineers playing the control board itself. Producer Phil Spector manufactured a series of hits with vocal groups such as the Ronettes, the Crystals, Bob B. Soxx and the Blue Jeans, and the Righteous Brothers by overdubbing their voices into "a wall of sound." The singers might have marginal natural talent, but with catchy pop hooks and multi-leveled orchestration, Spector's recordings garnered unprecedented sales and set new standards for the business.

As the decade went on, black music took a major step forward in its commercial success. Black artists and the black-based music business became more visible. The most obvious examples were Berry Gordy's Motown operation and the national rise of soul out of the fertile music scenes in Memphis, New Orleans, and Chicago. Quincy both catalyzed and benefited from the increased appreciation of African-American sounds, but ironically, it was his work with an unknown white teenager that brought him to the pinnacle of the pop world.

With his bebop pedigree, arranging credits, and European reputation, Quincy was widely hailed as a music maker, but not yet as a record seller. Few thought he could ever break through to the level of top-ten sales that Phil Spector had achieved, and he was constantly being ribbed by his Mercury co-workers for his failure to record "commercial" music. ▶ PG 115

ROD STEIGER
THE PAWNBROKER

I gave up my marriage and I gave up my job.

I LEFT NEW YORK AND JUST JUMPED IN.

After I did The Pawnbroker, I thought the offers were going to be rolling in, you know?

NOTHING. FOR TWO YEARS.

I guess part of it is the **ADVENTURE** and the **EXCITEMENT**, the **DANGER** of jumping into areas you don't really know... It's not really for real, but it is for real. And you can get back out.

–Quincy

"How's it working with a black man?"

I never think about that crap. Can you tell me what color a man is by just looking into his eyes? I doubt it.
—Richard Brooks

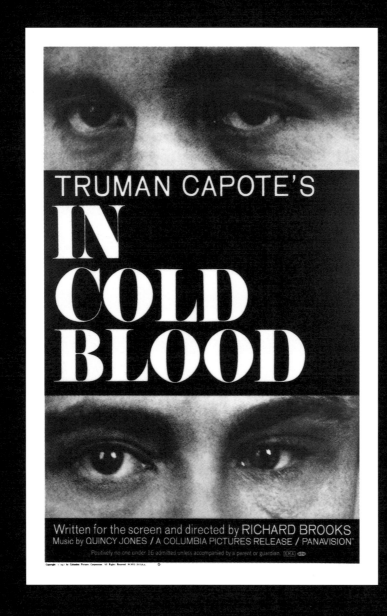

TRUMAN CAPOTE'S

IN COLD BLOOD

Written for the screen and directed by RICHARD BROOKS
Music by QUINCY JONES / A COLUMBIA PICTURES RELEASE / PANAVISION®

Positively no one under 16 admitted unless accompanied by a parent or guardian. [SMA] ⊕

Copyright © 1967 by Columbia Pictures Corporation. All Rights Reserved. PRINTED IN U.S.A. 🖐

Richard got tapes from the interrogation of the two kids. THE KILLERS. And that's where the score came fr

—just thinking like a murderer,

because you can do that as a composer. Just fall right in. —Quincy

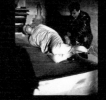

Rather than write music that tells the ear everything the eye is already seeing,

I let the ear go its own way and let the eye go its own way. –Quincy

Quincy wrote one of the best movie scores I'd ever heard, for In Cold Blood.

When I was 17 years old, I made a film in college, and I tracked the

entire picture with the In Cold Blood *score.* –Steven Spielberg

I went out to make *Mirage,* and

when I got there, they didn't know I

was **BLACK.** There were a lot

of startled people standing around.

They said,

"Excuse me

a minute, we'll

go in the

other room..."

GREGORY PECK IN "MIRAGE"

114

"MIRAGE"

Then at a staff meeting in the spring of 1963, Quincy and a group from the Mercury A&R team sat listening to the new batch of tapes submitted to Irvin Green that week, including one from a Long Island teenager. Quincy's ears immediately picked something up. "She was the first young artist that I'd heard sing in tune in a long time," he says, recalling his first impression of Lesley Gore. Their first record together, "It's My Party," launched a run of top-ten singles that included "Judy's Turn to Cry," "She's a Fool," "You Don't Own Me," "That's the Way Boys Are," "Maybe I Know," and "Sunshine, Lollipops, and Rainbows," which was the first Marvin Hamlisch composition to be recorded.

"Those were some of the first records with double voices," Quincy says. "Steve Lawrence had one with 'Go Away, Little Girl.' You had to do it then with the 'self-sync' process, and only a few engineers knew how. Phil Ramone was my engineer at the time, and he could do it." Ramone went on to produce many great albums by Billy Joel and Paul Simon, among others.

The Gore records demonstrated publicly and conclusively that Quincy was equally adept at creating mass-market hits and artistic successes. This was a jump almost no other bebopper had made, and it didn't sit well with some of Quincy's old colleagues, who accused Quincy of embracing just the kind of mass music and mass audience against which bebop had revolted. Quincy

...So Mancini, who was a long-

time friend, jumped in and said,

"Hey, guys,

get it together, this is the

20th century."

–Quincy

himself felt that he was merely broadening his scope and saw no conflict with his old jazzman persona. In fact, he continued his jazz efforts through the sixties. At the same time as the Gore records were released, he arranged several stellar big band–style recordings, including *It Might As Well Be Swing,* and a magnificent live album recorded in Las Vegas, *Swinging at the Sands,* both with Sinatra and Count Basie. He'd proven that he belonged with the best in jazz, then had equaled that achievement in pop. Now he turned to another dream and another medium.

1963: His First American Film Score, The Pawnbroker

As a child, Quincy had been enchanted by the music behind the glossy epics of Hollywood. As his credits as an arranger piled up, he began to

I WROTE THAT MUSIC FOR THE COTTON FIELD SCENE AND NORMAN JEWISON SAID,

"IT'S TOO ANGRY."

"IN THE HEAT OF THE NIGHT"

AND I SAID, "SHIT, I'M NOT SUPPOSED TO FEEL HAPPY ABOUT A COTTON FIELD." –QUINCY

think seriously about film composing as his next career move. The step was not an obvious one at the time. It would be years before the movie industry realized the creative possibilities of exploring (and exploiting) the music world's talent pool, and Quincy's swell of success got him nowhere in Hollywood. Grammys and gold records meant nothing to film studio executives.

As with Irvin Green and Mercury Records, it took another outsider to break the rules. Quincy scored his first American feature soundtrack for the independently produced film that marked the film debut of a celebrated television live-drama director, Sidney Lumet. Lumet was looking for a tough, somber sound for the tragic story of a man haunted by images of his life in Nazi Germany. Quincy got the job in part because he was good and in part because Lumet was married to the daughter of Quincy's good friend Lena Horne. Whatever the connection, the creation was startling, and *The Pawnbroker* was the first of three films Quincy would eventually score for Lumet.

1965: Los Angeles, Film Scores, Ironside Theme

The Pawnbroker set a new course for Quincy Jones. In 1965, he left Mercury and New York, determined to make his way in Los Angeles, in film. It was a brave and ambitious gesture; no black orchestrator or musician, not Basie, not Armstrong, not Ellington, had been ▶ PG 119

"IN THE HEAT OF THE NIGHT"

"In the heat of the night,

seems like a cold sweat

creepin' cross my brow.

In the heat of the night, I'm

feeling motherless somehow."

Quincy had seen me on **my little local talk show** *and wanted me to be* *Sofia.*

I don't think I would have gotten through it

had he not been there because it was undoubtedly the **MOST**

intimidating experience I've ever had.

—Oprah Winfrey

given more than an occasional score or featured cameo appearance in a Hollywood production. Quincy's first year in the West was predictably tough, but in 1965 he was finally hired by the producers of *Mirage,* a Gregory Peck vehicle for Universal. The studio executives didn't know Quincy was black, and when they found out, he almost lost the job. Happily, the producers' resolve and the protests of Quincy's friend and supporter Henry Mancini kept him on the job. Quincy's abilities quickly overcame the factor of prejudice, and more film and television work soon followed. His theme for NBC's *Ironside* was as brash and brassy as the show itself; it was also the first time anyone had used a synthesizer in arranging a television score.

From 1966 to 1969, Quincy spent much of his time in screening rooms, viewing rough cuts of motion pictures and television programs; his was often the only black face in a room of white filmmakers. In these early days of the civil rights movement, Quincy had few black colleagues in Hollywood, but he didn't have to walk entirely alone. Two other young black men were making Hollywood history, too. In 1965, Bill Cosby, a storytelling comic from Philadelphia, co-starred

119

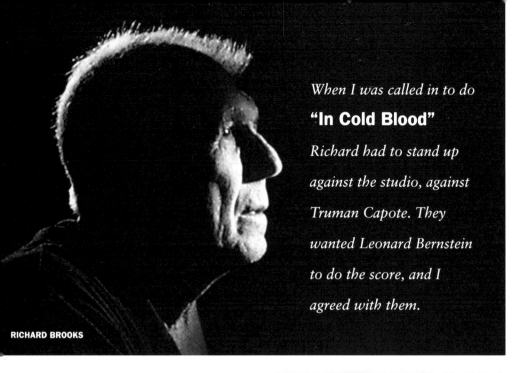

RICHARD BROOKS

When I was called in to do **"In Cold Blood"** *Richard had to stand up against the studio, against Truman Capote. They wanted Leonard Bernstein to do the score, and I agreed with them.*

This was not a black picture. And Richard said, **"Quincy's doing the score."** *It was not very common in 1968 in Hollywood.*
–*Quincy*

ALICE WALKER, QUINCY, STEVEN SPIELBERG

SIDNEY LUMET

...one of the fascinating things about Quincy is that he understands everything immediately. **He's completely curious.**
–*Sidney Lumet*

in NBC's *I Spy,* making him the first black dramatic actor to star in a television series. It launched a career that would eventually make him one of television's prime-time kings.

At the same time, a West Indian actor, Sidney Poitier, who'd won an Academy Award in 1963 for *Lilies of the Field,* was proving to incredulous studio execs that white audiences would pay to see a black leading man. He didn't dance or tell jokes, but had a cool, charismatic power no black actor had dared to display in American film. By 1967 Poitier was one of the nation's top box office attractions.

1967: In the Heat of the Night

Cosby, Poitier, and Jones were in the center of a mini civil rights movement in Hollywood. All three played key roles in destroying stereotypes of blacks on the screen and in the control room. They also made use of one another's talents. By the end of the decade, Quincy had scored four Poitier features, including *In the Heat of the Night, For Love of Ivy, The Lost Man,* and *Brother John,* and wrote the theme for Cosby's first sitcom on NBC in 1970.

Quincy drew on both his jazz and R&B background in his film compositions. "Alex North, Johnny Mandel, and Duke Ellington played around with utilizing jazz in film scoring, but Henry Mancini was clearly the pioneer there," Quincy has commented. "I feel I brought the sensibility of modern R&B influences into scoring, incorporating it in with the dramatic scoring. You have to get in there and cradle that drama, and you can't smother it. You can't jump all over it. It's a kind of hybrid art."

At first the work was everything he'd dreamed. He loved the challenge and the chance to innovate, to use large orchestras to heighten the humor in Goldie Hawn's *Cactus Flower* or the hipness of Paul Mazursky's *Bob & Carol & Ted & Alice*. He led an international life with his second wife, Ulla Anderson, splitting their time between London and Los Angeles. He spent New Year's Eve in London at Michael Caine's house with Roman Polanski and his wife, actress Sharon Tate. Back home, Billy Eckstine introduced him to a busy, Afroed aide to Dr. King; Quincy was immediately taken by the verve and energy of the young Jesse Jackson.

Despite the prestige and privilege of his Hollywood life, Quincy began to find film scoring stifling. Part of the job is, of course, to create the memorable theme that gives the film its aural trademark. That was fun and challenging. But it also involves looking after all the little bites of sound that underscore the action or bolster a scene that might not be working dramatically—or might need to be ground out to meet a distribution schedule. These aspects of the work can quickly become creative straitjackets or leave the composer feeling like a small cog in a very big machine. Quincy wanted to be the driving force at the center of the musical action again, and that meant going back into the recording studio.

1969: Walking in Space

In 1969, the year the New York Mets came out of nowhere to capture the World Series, Quincy made his own minor miracle in New York. "I was on a two-week hiatus between films, so I went to New York, gathered all the cats together, and wrote and recorded an album in about ten days," Quincy remembers. *Walking in Space* featured Bob James on keyboard, trumpeter Freddie Hubbard, Hubert Laws on flute, saxophonist Roland Kirk, and singer-songwriter Valerie Simpson, a celebrated Motown tunesmith who made her debut as a recording artist on this album. "Killer Joe," his interpretation of the Edwin Hawkins Singers' "Oh Happy Day," and the title song, taken from the countercultural

I thought a BLACK director really should be doing *The Color Purple* and Quincy said to me, "Did you have to go to OUTER SPACE and hire a superior intelligence to direct a movie about an ALIEN?" —Steven Spielberg

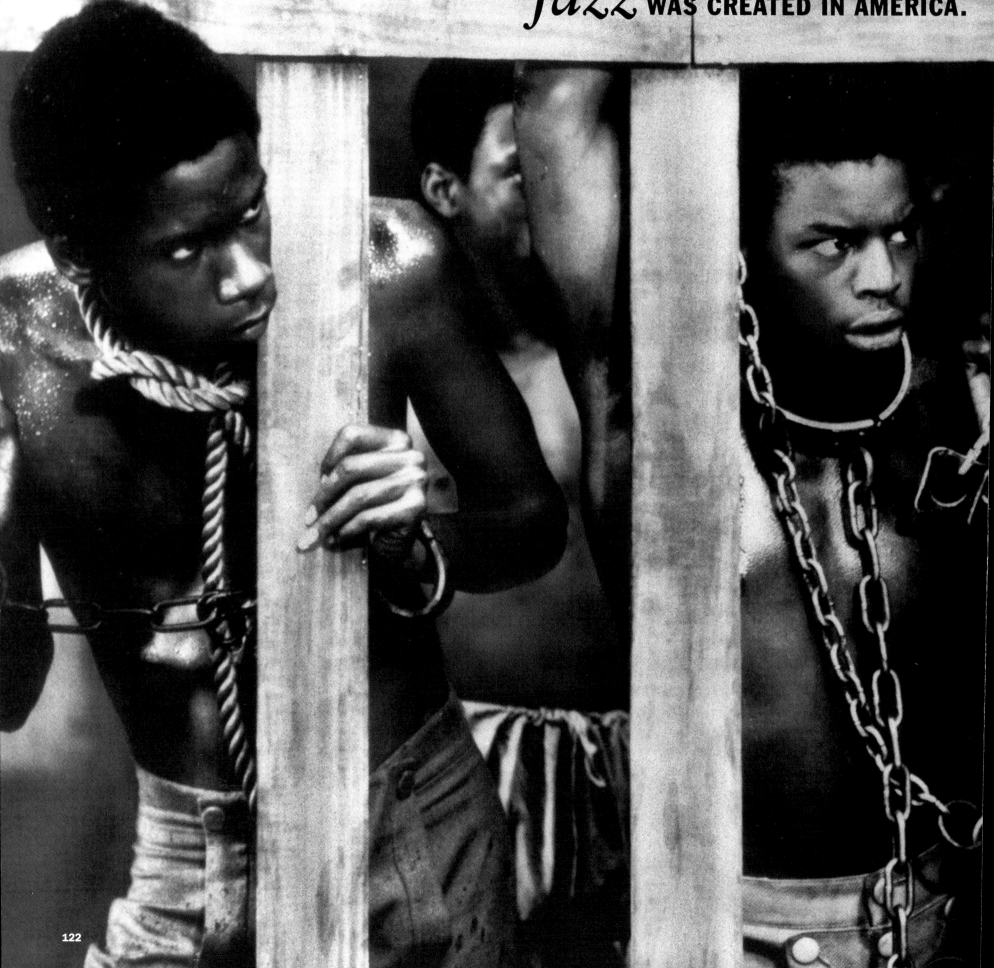

Jazz WAS CREATED IN AMERICA.

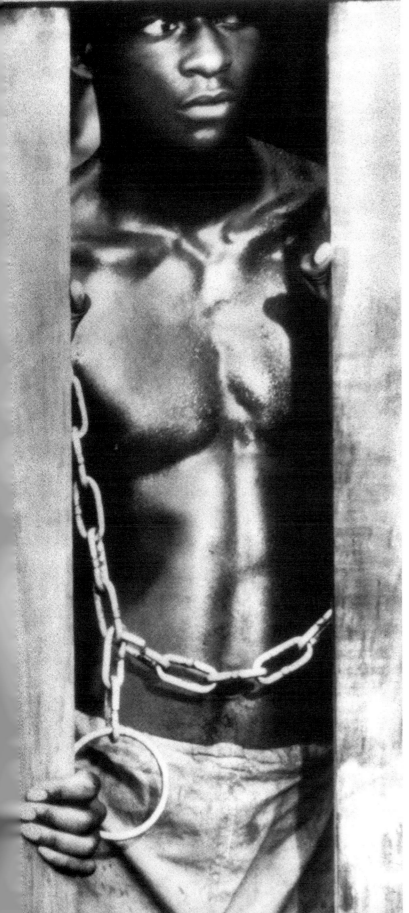

NOT THROUGH ANY GREAT EDUCATIONAL FORCE,

BUT FROM THE *souls* OF PEOPLE WHO WERE BROUGHT HERE UNDER *protest.*

—DIZZY GILLESPIE

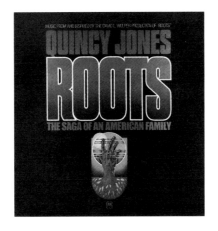

musical *Hair*, highlighted the collection. The horns still blared, demonstrating Quincy's ongoing love for the big sound, but it also featured the distinctive Fender Rhodes electric piano, which with the synthesizer was changing the textures of contemporary music. *Walking* won a Grammy as the best jazz performance by a large group, and ended the decade for Quincy on a grand note; he was back in the saddle as a record maker.

1974: Body Heat, operations

In the summer of 1974, Quincy Jones was at a peak. He had a new love, television star Peggy Lipton; his new album, *Body Heat*, was the best selling in his career. But he was struggling under the weight of crushing, lingering head pains that signaled the presence of an aneurysm, a bubble-like defect in the artery that supplies blood to the right side of the brain. The bubble finally ruptured, spilling blood at the base of the brain. "It felt like someone had shot off the back of my head," Quincy recalls. "After a while, it seemed as if I could actually hear and feel the blood sloshing around in there. It was as if the life was leaking out of my body." He packed two operations into his schedule like extra recording sessions. In August the surgeons went inside his head to correct the aneurysm. In September he married Peggy Lipton and was feted by A & M Records to celebrate *Body Heat*'s going gold at 500,000 sold. In October, the doctors operated a second time, inserting pins to hold his skull in place. He was forbidden to play the trumpet again. The pressure would be too great. Doctors also suggested he go back home, take it easy, rest up. He did, but not for very long.

1975: Gula Matari, Smackwater Jack

Before the operations, Quincy had plunged into a new frenzy of composing. He was on a roll with electronic, synthesized rhythm-based music, and nothing—not one operation or two—was ▶ PG 126

In 1968, after Dr. King was **ASSASSINATED** and there was a great **FUROR** and a great **TENSION,** Quincy came back home to Chicago and sought me out. He felt a need to address himself to *the agony* of that period. — Jesse Jackson

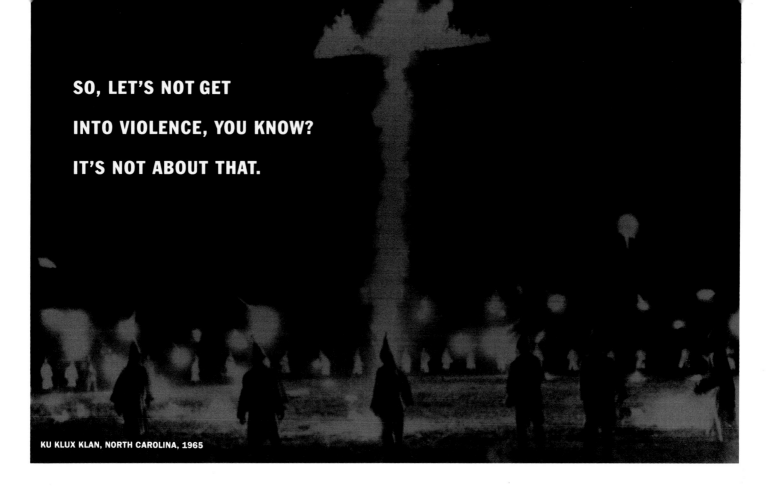

SO, LET'S NOT GET
INTO VIOLENCE, YOU KNOW?
IT'S NOT ABOUT THAT.

KU KLUX KLAN, NORTH CAROLINA, 1965

It's about recycling energy.

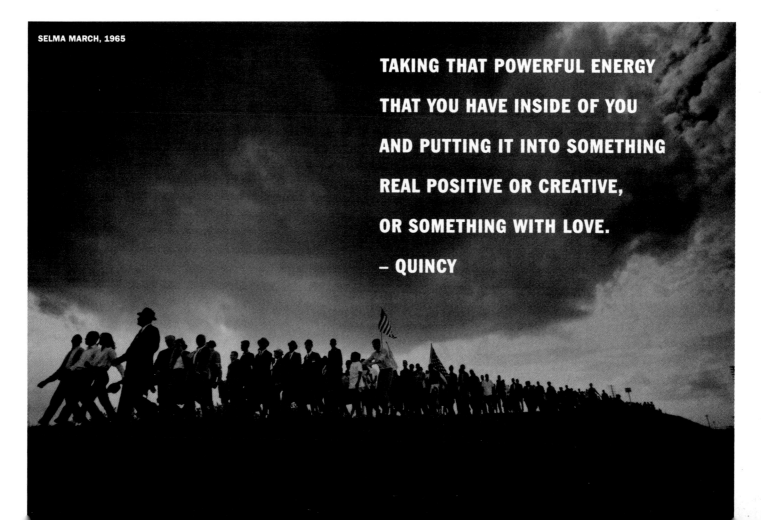

SELMA MARCH, 1965

TAKING THAT POWERFUL ENERGY
THAT YOU HAVE INSIDE OF YOU
AND PUTTING IT INTO SOMETHING
REAL POSITIVE OR CREATIVE,
OR SOMETHING WITH LOVE.
– QUINCY

going to keep him away for long. *Body Heat* had succeeded because Quincy, for the first time in his career as a recording artist, had sold to the R&B-loving audience. It completed a transition that had begun with *Walking in Space* and continued through *Gula Matari, Smackwater Jack,* and *You've Got It Bad, Girl.* He'd shed another part of his jazz-only identification; now he could get in his licks as an R&B pop artist, too.

It was a deliberate move on Quincy's part, and the right one for the times. The early seventies were a golden era in black popular music as black musicians, inspired by the political strides of the sixties and the black pride movement, expanded the technical and lyrical scope of their music. Singles broke the conventional three-minute limit for black pop; black listeners began to buy albums on a mass scale. Lyricists tackled other topics besides love and dancing; social commentary in song, supported by new instrumental textures from the third world—congas, bongos, the kalimba—became popular. Technology in the form of the wahwah pedal for guitars, the electric piano, and the Moog synthesizer made radically new sounds from those of the soul era. The top explorers of the new sound included Marvin Gaye, Donny Hathaway, Norman Whitfield, Kenny Gamble, Leon Huff—but Stevie Wonder, without question, dominated the movement. Wonder had grown from a child star to a creative force equally adept at songwriting, singing, and producing. Quincy felt Wonder made music that defied category, writing in 1976, "How to classify Stevie Wonder's 'Too High'? It cannot be called rhythm and blues. He plays polytonal chords and jazz figures along with rhythm and blues licks; it's a total fusion. Harmonically, melodically, and every other way, it really has a jazz base, but it is performed by artists who are categorized as rhythm and blues."

After *In the Heat of the Night,* he started talking to me about getting tired of doing movie scores.

I was doing up to eight

He's quite right. I think that if a composer concentrates

movies a year...I must

solely on movies, he's going to lose something inside

have done thirty-four,

himself and in his work. Talk about low man on the

thirty-eight films...

totem pole—composers are more violated in their

—Quincy

work than writers are. —Sidney Lumet

broker Walk Don't Run
Mirage
nter Laughing
e Heat Of The Night
Cold Blood The Cosby
Gold
Mystery Theme
Carol and Ted and Alice
Mary Cactus Flower
ster Tibbs
s. The Hot Rock
etaway For Love of Ivy
y Landlord The Wiz
e City The Color Purple
Oprah Winfrey Show

> THE SPROCKETS DON'T LIE, THAT'S THE HARD PART. IF THE MOVIE WOULD CHANGE EVERY TIME YOU CHANGED THE MUSIC, YOU'D BE IN GREAT SHAPE. BUT IT DOESN'T. YOU'RE THERE WITH A FIXED AMOUNT OF TIME THAT WILL NOT BEND, BREAK OR SPLINTER. IT'S A PREDETERMINED DRAMATIC STRUCTURE THAT YOU'RE STUCK WITH.
> —QUINCY

1975: The Brothers Johnson

It's not surprising that a Wonder tune, "You've Got It Bad, Girl," provided the title for one Quincy album, and *Body Heat* was very much influenced by Wonder's harmonic and melodic approach. *Body Heat* also showed that Quincy's ear for new talent was still keen. Al Jarreau and Minnie Riperton, both of whom went on to solo stardom, provided the vocals. Two songs he selected for the album became seventies standards: Bernard Ighner's "Everything Must Change" and "If I Ever Lose This Heaven," written by Leon Ware and Pam Sawyer.

Early in 1975, Quincy began to make plans for a three-week Japanese tour and launched pre-production on his next album, *Mellow Madness*, but in February, he hit a snag. The busy schedules of Los Angeles's top players were making it tough to get far on either project. Joe Greene, a road manager and friend, suggested Quincy meet with two young brothers he knew, Louis and George Johnson. These L.A. natives had been playing professionally since adolescence, both with their own band and behind pros like Little Richard. Louis was a phenomenon on bass, especially adept at slapping strings with his thumb to create a thick, funky bottom. George was a smart guitar player with a good ear for melody and a smooth, crooning singing style. They were overjoyed at the prospect of meeting Quincy; but neither could read music, and they feared they'd embarrass themselves in front of the great man.

They had nothing to worry about. Quincy thought their sound was so full of untapped promise that he took them on as protégés, much as Clark Terry and Ray Charles had once done for him. On the plane to and from Japan, in rehearsals, and even on the bandstand, Quincy gave the brothers a crash course in music theory. And as before, it wasn't a one-sided relationship. In Japan, George wrote a song called "Is It Love That We're Missin'?," a mid-tempo love ▶ PG 130

producer

ballad that Quincy adored. He discovered that
they had a complete catalogue of finished songs,
melodic ideas, and rhythmic licks. Four of the
songs ended up on *Mellow Madness,* with "Is It
Love?" released as the first single.

After the album was completed, the three
men sat down and went through the Johnsons'
entire collection—over 200 compositions. The
most promising material formed the backbone of
the Brothers Johnsons' 1975 debut, *Look Out
for #1*. The album was a multi-layered hit with
airplay on pop, black, and jazz radio. "I'll Be
Good to You" was a top-ten pop and black chart
single; "Get the Funk Outta Ma Face" became a
dance anthem, and the instrumental "Thunder
Thumbs and Lightning Licks" appealed to mellow jazz fans. With Quincy as producer, the
Brothers Johnson became consistent hit makers,
garnering platinum sales with their first album

When I did *Walking in*

Space, I just wanted to

get away from movies for

a while — get away from

the restrictions of synchro-

nization and being locked

up in a studio. I just

wanted to paint a canvas

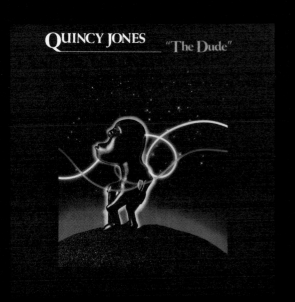

that would have all of my

favorite musicians on it

and just sail, with

no ropes

to tie you to the ground. –Quincy

THERE ARE SOME PRODUCERS THAT DON'T KNOW ENOUGH, AND YOU KNOW YOU'RE
THRILL HIM. —BARBRA STREISAND

PULLING THE WOOL OVER THEIR EYES, YOU'RE NOT DOING YOUR BEST. SOMEHOW

YOU JUST WANT TO PLEASE HIM, YOU WANT TO IMPRESS HIM, YOU WANT TO

YOU JUST DON'T HAVE THE NEED TO PLEASE THEM. QUINCY HAS THAT AURA—

and three later hits, *Right on Time, Light Up the Night,* and *Blam!*

1977: Roots and The Wiz

Ironically, just as Quincy's commercial clout as producer and artist was gaining momentum, two projects detoured him back into scoring: the 1977 ABC mini-series *Roots* and, in the next year, *The Wiz,* Universal's all-black musical version of *The Wizard of Oz. Roots* brought to television the monumental story of Alex Haley's search for his family's path from Africa to and through America. Haley and Jones had been friends since the latter's days at Mercury, in New York. The series eventually captured the highest ratings in TV history. Quincy's stirring score used African chants and rhythms to underscore the story of the destruction of a society by the institution of slavery. Quincy says his chief regret was that the producers didn't allow him to use as much traditional African music as he'd have liked. Still, the score for *Roots* was the first time most Americans, black or white, had heard music that explicitly linked African sounds with styles indigenous to the U.S. "African music had always been regarded in the West as primitive and savage, but when you take the time to really study it, you see that it's as structured and sophisticated as European classical music, with the same basic components as you'll find in a symphony orchestra—instruments that are plucked, instruments that are beaten, and instruments that are blown with reeds. And it's music from the soil—powerful, elemental…From gospel, blues, jazz, soul, R&B, rock'n'roll, all the way to rap, you can trace the roots straight back to Africa."

The Wiz was a project brought to Quincy by his old chum, director Sidney Lumet, and Quincy did a professional job though he wasn't a fan of the original music from the Broadway production. While neither an artistic nor commercial success, *The Wiz* did introduce two people whose later collaborations would redefine the ▶ PG 136

And when they have enough

trust in you to take the CHANCE,

with no net, no parachute,

it's a little SCARY

and maybe a little PAINFUL,

but that's when

the good stuff happens.

—Quincy

FRANK SINATRA AT THE SANDS, 1965

▲ HERBIE HANCOCK

▲ JAMES INGRAM

▲ PEGGY LEE

▲ SAMMY DAVIS, JR.

▲ RINGO STARR ▲ JOSÉ FELICIANO

▲ PAUL SIMON

MY INSTRUMENT

is playing all of these things. Playing the **SINGERS,**

playing the **SONGS,** *playing the* **MUSICIANS,**

and seeing that big vision.

It's like a huge canvas. **A TAPESTRY.** *–Quincy*

▲ MICHAEL JACKSON

▲ QUINCY, ELLA FITZGERALD, BARBRA STREISAND

▼ RAY CHARLES

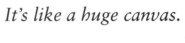

▲ MANHATTAN TRANSFER

▼ AL JARREAU

▼ LESLEY GORE   ▲ DIANA ROSS

◄ QUINCY WITH THE BROTHERS JOHNSON

There is

an expression

I always use in the studio:

You have

to leave room for

MARK KIBBLE, MERVYN WARREN OF TAKE 6

to walk through the room.

GOD

–Quincy

McCartney ("Girlfriend"), Tom Bahler ("She's Out of My Life") and Heatwave member Rod Temperton ("Rock with You"), beautifully framed by engineer Bruce Swedien, complemented Jackson's perky title track and the album's masterpiece, "Don't Stop Till You Get Enough." Fueled by Michael's soon-to-be-trademark "woo's," frisky rhythms, and intricate horn and string charts, "Don't Stop" was an instant classic.

Without the success of *Off the Wall*, there would have been no *Thriller* or *Bad*. Made in the years before Jackson could exploit his dancing talents in music videos, *Off the Wall* had to be exceptional musically to sell the then-amazing seven million copies. Back in 1983, Quincy noted, "Michael has got all you need emotionally, but he backs it up with discipline and pacing. He'll never burn himself out because he's always on the case about knowing his direction and how he'd like to grow. He'd come in during *Off the Wall* and put down two lead vocals and three background parts in one day. He does his homework. Most singers want to do everything in the studio. They're lazy. Michael Jackson is going to be the biggest star of the eighties and nineties." It's crucial to remember Quincy said this before *Thriller*.

1984: Thriller

Right in the white-hot center of the videoactive, computerized, digital eighties, Quincy Jones lived large. He had come a long way from having to fight to arrange the string section of an orchestra—his plate was now as full as it could be. He left A & M and formed his own label, Qwest, at Warner Bros. In 1981 he and his protégés James Ingram and Patti Austin produced a single, "Baby, Come to Me," that climbed to number one; he won the Grammy for Producer of the Year the same year for his solo album, *The Dude*, and another Grammy for his recording of Lena Horne's Broadway show. He was a significant money raiser for Jesse Jackson's two ▶ PG 144

I think he really belongs to

The career seemed to be the

the world. As a woman you

given, the steady. So, whatever

have to know that. You have

happened, I always ran for

to feel that he is not really all

that, because that would

yours and could never be. The price which

My third marriage

never let me down. –Quincy

that exacts in a relation-

...well, Peggy was

ship is a very heavy one.

different. –Quincy

–Oprah Winfrey

QUINCY AND PEGGY LIPTON

2 ▷ 2A   3 ▷ 3A   4 ▷ 4A

I just kept screaming, "Help! Help me!" It was an aneurysm. The brain was so damaged and

8 ▷ 8A   9 ▷ 9A   10 ▷ 10A

It was equivalent to sixteen strokes. Like a hose with the water full force, and you let it loose,

14 ▷ 14A   15 ▷ 15A   16 ▷ 16A

5 ▷ 5A   **6** ▷ 6A   **7** ▷ 7A

swollen, if they went in then, it would have just jumped straight out of my head...

11 ▷ 11A   **12** ▷ 12A   **13** ▷ 13A

it just goes all over the place. Like somebody just shot the whole back of your head out.

17 ▷ 17A   **18** ▷ 18A   **19** ▷ 19A

historic runs for the Democratic nomination for President. But Quincy's decade was only beginning.

Michael Jackson's gyrating body and ringing high-pitched tones of course dominate our memories of *Thriller*, but it's equally important to remember the immense contribution of Quincy and his musical family to the album's phenomenal achievement. While Michael composed the two breakthrough singles, "Billie Jean" and "Beat It," Quincy called on the skills of longtime associates Rod Temperton ("Thriller," "Baby, Be Mine," "Lady in My Life") and singer James Ingram ("P.Y.T. [Pretty Young Thing]") to strengthen the selections. Louis Johnson played bass on most of the album. Swedien's engineering was a masterpiece that balanced the need for a clean sound with the dramatic demands of Michael's vocal performances. Quincy supervised Michael and his comrades, constantly driving toward quality by attending to detail. Consider how "Billie Jean" was recorded. Quincy made Louis Johnson play four different basses on the track before he was satisfied with his tone; Johnson's explosive riff underpins the song. Then he recorded a number of drummers before deciding to mix Ndugu Chancler's live sound and a drum machine. For a final bit of sweetening, Quincy hired saxophonist Tom Scott to add a lyrical solo. "It was Quincy's idea to weave this little thread into the thing," says Swedien. "It was a last-minute overdub. Quincy calls it ear candy. You're not conscious of it. It's just a subliminal element that works well." This extraordinary level of craftsmanship fueled *Thriller*'s chart-smashing rise and helped make it a musical landmark.

1985: We Are the World

Quincy's success with Michael Jackson and his unique track record with a wide range of performers made him the only possible choice to produce the 1985 all-star benefit album

NOVEMBER, 1974, QUINCY SHORTLY AFTER ANEURYSM

The rough one was the second time.

Only one in a hundred makes it.

I've taken a lot of time from my children that should have been their time in order to put it into my creative outlet. And it feels **SELFISH** to me

TINA

KIDADA

I don't know whether you've ever seen him write,

but he gets his head kind of cocked, as if the **notes**

were **stabbing him** in the back.

The only way you could really *get to him*

was to hit a chord in a different key. –Lloyd Jones

QUINCY III

RASHIDA

KIDADA, PEGGY LIPTON, AND QUINCY

He was so **fatherlike** and so **HELPFUL.** *We built a camaraderie that was like a father-son type of friendship;* *he was always to the rescue and very* **loving.** *He has a very fatherlike charm. That's the main thing that's unique to him.*

–Michael Jackson

QUINCY, RASHIDA, QUINCY III, AND KIDADA

QUINCY AND KIDADA

This last divorce, from my third marriage, really affected me very strongly, emotionally. It made me reassess my essence as a human being. –Quincy *He didn't see things coming until they were right on top of him. –Jolie Jones Levine* Usually, I've been so involved in my work that I just keep in motion, without thinking about other things. –Quincy *The life just went right out of the house. I know it happens each time. It happened to both sets of other children...The phone stops ringing, people don't come over any more. –Jolie Jones Levine* If the family thing happens to suffer from it, I just don't think it's something that he has any control over. –Lloyd Jones *Music is very self-centered. You have to tune everything else out. It's hard to share...And sharing is what marriage is all about. –Bobby Tucker*

I hated

doing *The Wiz.* I did not want
to do it. Sidney knew that, too.

I didn't like the music, you
know? And I didn't like the
script. –Quincy

Quincy kept referring to it as
"polishing shit." –Sidney Lumet

If I hadn't done *The Wiz,*
I wouldn't have worked with

Michael, you know? –Quincy

that became *We Are the World.* The enormous effort, inspired by Bob Geldof's U.K. megastar recording "Do They Know It's Christmas?," was coordinated by artist manager Ken Kragen under the banner of the organization USA for Africa, to raise money for famine relief in Ethiopia. Kragen was hoping to corral even more stars than Geldof had, and to do so he needed a producer with great credibility as well as talent-managing skills: Quincy Jones.

Shortly after the 1985 American Music Awards show, forty of the biggest names in pop music gathered in a recording studio in L.A. to turn their attention to a song written by Michael Jackson and Lionel Richie. Bruce Springsteen, Stevie Wonder, Billy Joel, Paul Simon, Diana Ross, Cyndi Lauper, and Willie Nelson were there, and they'd only be available for one session. There was no time for retakes, and it had to work.

"It's a terrifying responsibility," Quincy recalls. "Terrifying because it's just enormous, an enormous canvas. People there are very original individuals, beautiful, soulful human beings." The session went smoothly, due in large part to the talents of the man running the show. Quincy simply stood up in front of a room packed with the world's multi-million-selling singers, a big band of voices comparable to the great horn sections of Basie and Hampton, and, as usual, played their tonations and styles expertly.

The double jolts of *Thriller* and *We Are the World* gave Quincy clear and sole claim to the title of preeminent pop producer in the world. But while these two blockbusters might have capped another's musical career, they signaled no end to the inexhaustible Quincy Jones's creative efforts. As the mammoth hits were playing around the world, Quincy returned to movie making, but in the new role of producer.

1986: The Color Purple

Alice Walker's novel *The Color Purple* told the story of two black sisters in the rural South victimized by racism and male chauvinism. It became one of the literary events of the decade. Many black men denounced it as a stereotyped assault on their manhood and on the black family. Yet millions of readers found that Walker had tapped into themes of male domination and racial injustice that were both specific to the black community and that resonated in the experiences of people from all kinds of backgrounds. To Quincy, the emotional truth of the story overwhelmed any other objections. It was simply a work of art, and he was determined to bring it to the screen. Peter Guber owned the rights to the book, and Quincy's sheer passion convinced Guber to let him co-produce it; that same commitment eventually wooed Steven Spielberg into directing it.

Quincy's decision to go after a director known for his glossy, suburban—and white—movies shocked many. To Quincy, however, Spielberg was a director uniquely capable of pairing universal emotions with a panoramic visual style. Just twenty years before, Quincy'd been struggling to land soundtrack jobs. Now, through the power of his personality and passion, he was able to sign on the best-known director in the nation. And he didn't stop there. It was Quincy who spotted Oprah Winfrey on television while visiting Chicago and immediately saw her big-screen potential. Winfrey's role as Sophia in *The Color Purple* helped launch her toward national celebrity.

For Quincy the artist, life could hardly get sweeter. But for Quincy the private man, the period following these huge successes was the most traumatic since his operations in 1974. ▶ PG 154

We did the movie and after the movie, out of total honesty and total sincerity, I called Quincy up and said, "I'm going to do an album, can you recommend any **PRODUCERS?"**

I was not trying to hint, I was not trying to beg him. He said, "Gee, why don't you **LET ME DO IT."** *I said, "Oh,* **WOW!** *That's great." It was funny, because I never thought about that. —Michael Jackson*

I told him that I had something but I didn't want to play it

"THRILLER" SOLD

for him. And so he forced me to drive to my house, he

FORTY MILLION ALBUMS.

forced me to get the engineer and to do the song. I was

there singing my heart out to this song, and when it was

FORTY MILLION!

over, he just loved it. He said, "That was just the song that

–QUINCY

we were looking for." It was "Beat It." –Michael Jackson

He just, you know, he just *SHOT* him off the launch pad.

This is the first

time kids around

the world ever had

a black hero.

—Quincy

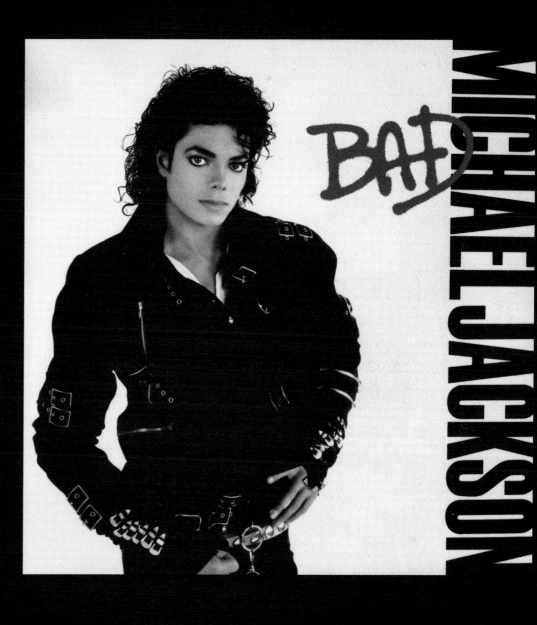

MICHAEL JACKSON

BAD

BOOM!

—Melle Mel

They've both got such

gaiety; *the* **laughter,** *the*

jolliness. *But none of*

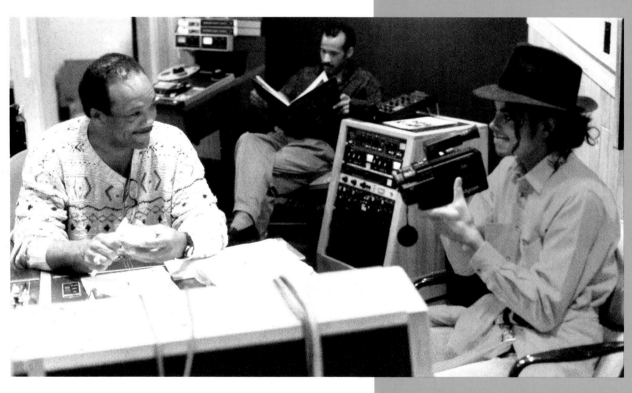

that changes the fact

that, in my view, they

are **open wounds.**

– Sidney Lumet

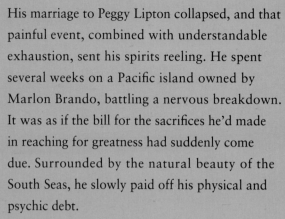

His marriage to Peggy Lipton collapsed, and that painful event, combined with understandable exhaustion, sent his spirits reeling. He spent several weeks on a Pacific island owned by Marlon Brando, battling a nervous breakdown. It was as if the bill for the sacrifices he'd made in reaching for greatness had suddenly come due. Surrounded by the natural beauty of the South Seas, he slowly paid off his physical and psychic debt.

Back in Los Angeles, Quincy focused on developing more film projects—a biography of the African-Russian writer Pushkin obsessed him. He worked with Michael Jackson on *Bad* and finally attacked his next solo album. It had been nearly a decade since *The Dude*. The excuses for the gap were valid, but the longer he waited, the greater the pressure would mount to create not just something good but a grand, glorious statement. The artistic inspiration for this culminating project would come, as it turned out, from a most unlikely group of entertainers. ▶ PG 156

Michael Jackson is one of the world's great entertainers.

I first started to work with him in '78, and at that stage—Michael had been in the business since he was five years old—he had almost had fifteen years' experience, very disciplined experience. But when we get in a room, and he's singing me a new song, I have to turn the lights out and put my hands over my eyes and let him sit behind the couch. Yet in front of ninety thousand people he turns into an animal.

Michael has been on a journey that very few mortals will ever experience. I've been to Europe with him, I've been to Japan and all over the United States, and to see just what that feels like physically...it's a lot of energy coming towards one person. A lot of energy. And it's not human at all, it's got nothing to do with anything normal. For somebody that's been in the public eye since he's five years old and then have this happen on top of it, I don't know how anybody could expect him to be Mr. Joe Next Door. That's not going to happen. –Q

Michael Jackson

He redefined how far a black artist can go.

All my life, I wanted to see an entertainer like Michael really do his thing with no limitations, no boundaries, no preconceived ideas about what he should do, how far he should go, or anything.

He'll make you do a thing over and over. He tries to see what you can do, how versatile you are, even if it's embarrassing. And it can be very embarrassing.

—Michael Jackson

—Quincy

1986: Hip Hop

Canastel's is a spacious, chic Italian restaurant on Park Avenue South in Manhattan. It's a yuppie haven where suited Young Turks toss down martinis and count the rungs they've climbed that day on the corporate ladder. The clientele is white and decidedly moneyed: not a place where the urban street culture usually intrudes. But on a night in December 1986 the street walked in.

When Quincy Jones and his son Snoopy arrived, the crowd was pleased. It was good to know famous musicians ate here. But who were those other guys? Trailing behind the Joneses was a long line of young African-Americans sporting unlaced sneakers, gold chains of varying thickness, baseball caps, and sweat suits. They walked with as much rhythm as any jive record. It was Snoopy's eighteenth birthday, and with the help of top rap manager Russell Simmons, Quincy had come up with a fabulous birthday present: an evening with the country's top rap stars— Run DMC, L.L.Cool J., the Beastie Boys, Whodini and the Fat Boys. Gathering in the far corner of the shocked, chic restaurant, the party kept growing as friends of the family and rappers piled in.

Snoopy, who grew up in Sweden, was a rap fanatic, and he had suggested that his father get in touch with Simmons and find out for himself what this new revolt in tune was all about. It was a momentous encounter when the architect of the high-tech pop sound met with the makers of records whose raw edges were a direct reaction to precisely that managed sound on the radio. Hip hop, built around the rhymes of performers and sonic collages of beats by deejays manipulating turntables, had blossomed out of New York and was spreading across the country. Some adults of all races criticized the music for its ultra-macho, unmelodic core and for its negative images—it seemed like ugly noise to them. Snoopy was eager to know what ▶ PG 163

Tevin Campbell
is like a signal. Because I
remember meeting
Stevie Wonder
at the Apollo Theatre,
when he was twelve years
old. And you could feel
that thing in him. I
remember meeting
Michael Jackson
at Sammy Davis's house,
when he was twelve years
old. And you could feel
that thing. And when I
first saw the video of
Tevin, he had that same
thing—we haven't seen
that combination of a
great voice and dancing
ability in a while. It'll be
very interesting to see
what happens when his
voice changes, because
that's something you
always have to consider.
But it didn't bother Stevie
and Michael.
–Quincy

157

THIS IS WHEN A PERSON THAT DOESN'T BELIEVE IN A HIGHER POWER HAS GOT TO BE A LITTLE BENT,

BECAUSE THERE ARE TOO MANY *things that came together* FOR IT JUST TO BE AN ACCIDENT.

159

I didn't realize how **HEAVY** it was. I don't think anybody did, until he had to *go away*.

It was a strange postcard. It...he told us how much he missed us, how much he loved us, and that he's been trying to write this card for ten days. And I...I thought, "Boy," you know, "he must really be having a hard time."

– Jolie Jones Levine

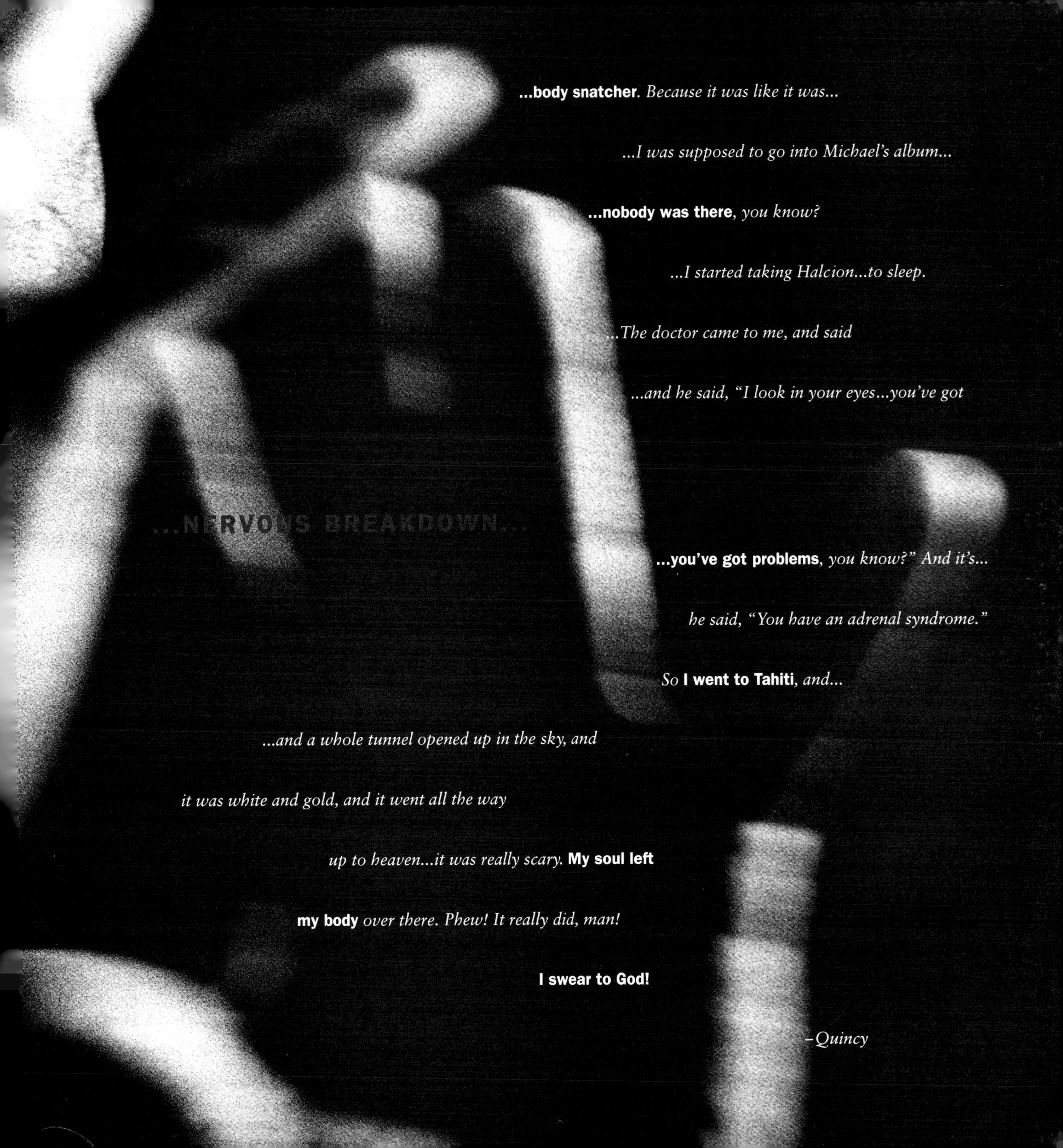

...body snatcher. *Because it was like it was...*

...I was supposed to go into Michael's album...

...nobody was there, *you know?*

...I started taking Halcion...to sleep.

...The doctor came to me, and said

...and he said, "I look in your eyes...you've got

...NERVOUS BREAKDOWN...

...you've got problems, *you know?" And it's...*

he said, "You have an adrenal syndrome."

So I went to Tahiti, *and...*

...and a whole tunnel opened up in the sky, and

it was white and gold, and it went all the way

up to heaven...it was really scary. **My soul left**

my body *over there. Phew! It really did, man!*

I swear to God!

–Quincy

Quincy decided to let

Michael and I have a meeting

to go ahead and

put the song together.

–Lionel Richie

QUINCY RECORDING "WE ARE THE WORLD"

162

Quincy would make of it all.

He loved it. He looked at hip hop's contempt for authority, racial injustice, and conventional codes of conduct, as well as the rappers' distinctive language and dress, and saw himself and the other members of the bebop fraternity from the fifties coming alive again. There were substantial differences in sound and demeanor between the beboppers and hip hoppers, but characteristically,

the bebop with a dash of hip hop; the power of the gospel choir; the lush vocals of a Zulu chant; a taste of jazz; an a cappella celebration—each and all evoking tears and laughter."

The album doesn't merely offer samples from his long career, but attempts to fuse all his styles into one musical statement. The opening rap duet speaks directly to that theme of synthesis. The effect is heightened by the title song,

"Guys, I need a hit record."

Quincy didn't focus on what separated these generations of outlaw black musicians, but on what united them.

For years Quincy had talked of recording a multi-record set that would chronicle the history of African-American music from its roots in West Africa right up to the latest sounds from the street. As he began to focus his attention on his solo album in 1988 and 1989, hip hop, with its rhythmic intensity and storytelling components, became a central style in the project. He called the record *Back on the Block,* and its prologue is composed of raps by Quincy Jones Junior and Jones the Third—aka Snoopy—performing together. The elder's efforts may not have overwhelmed the more accomplished rappers, but it showed how keen Quincy was to keep experimenting, even to risk failing, in pursuit of a new sound.

"I've traveled many paths the past forty years of playing, composing, arranging, and producing music—and at last—*Back on the Block* is something I've always dreamed of doing," he wrote on the liner notes. "Each and all of those who are joined together here have a special meaning to me. Together with our friendship, we share the traditions of the African griot storyteller which are continued today by the rappers; the sensuous harmonies within Brazilian music;

Those were our marching orders. –Lionel Richie

But when Lionel and I get together we just play and tell stories and laugh all day. For the first day, we goofed off, and Quincy was calling: "Where's the song? Where's the song?"
–Michael Jackson

The first night we met we did everything but write a song. Well, the next two nights Quincy came to dinner and there was still no song. And finally he said, "Listen, I have 45 artists waiting to hear this song they've agreed to sing that they have no idea what they're going to sing, and you've got to give it to me tomorrow."
–Lionel Richie

which combines raps by Ice-T, Melle Mel, Big Daddy Kane, and Kool Moe Dee with lead vocals by twelve-year-old singer Tevin Campbell and booming harmonies from a choir conducted by gospel great Andrae Crouch on lyrics written by the African musician Caiphus Semenya. "I Don't Go for That" and "One Man Woman," co-written and arranged by Ian Prince and featuring lead vocals by Quincy's longtime protégé Siedah Garrett, are the kind of bright, crystal-clear pop anthems that have been Quincy's trademark since the mid-seventies.

Track by track, the album carries you across a musical history, with a powerful cumulative effect. Reaching back to the Brothers Johnson's first album, Quincy re-recorded two of its most popular cuts, "I'll Be Good to You" and "Tomorrow." For his update of "I'll Be Good," Quincy united two great vocalists, Ray Charles and Chaka Khan. "Tomorrow" had originally been an instrumental, but Garrett, who'd co-written the smash hit "Man in the Mirror," wrote lyrics which Quincy used to showcase the sensational sound of young Tevin Campbell, backed by a children's choir. Quincy's ongoing fascination with Brazilian music and culture was apparent in "Setembro," by Ivan Lins and Gilson Peranzzetta; vocals by the quartet Take 6 and Sarah Vaughan stand as another ▶ PG 168

Music **IS A FAMILY...EVERYONE'S JOINED IN IT.**

Music is a strange animal, because

no matter what the political context is,

you can't stop music from coming in. –Quincy

I'M GLAD TO BE PART OF THAT *family*.–QUINCY

Melle Mel

Every time I would try to go to the wrong side, that's what would always ring in my head:

I first turned on to rap through two sources: The Last Poets and African Litigation ceremonies. The ceremonies are almost like musical ritual with call and response. • Rap roots also come from the griots, groups of singing troubadours who travel from town to town spreading news and awareness. They're like singing musical poets who are oral historians. They say that every time a griot dies a volume of history goes, too. Rappers haven't known they come from these traditions.

• Rappers are the best role models we have. Every rapper I know is clean as chitlins. They have determination, pride, and hungry, inquisitive minds. Their word power is growing.

• Rap will cross over because 14 year old white kids always need new forms of vitality and rebelliousness. Right now that's coming from hip hop.

'Rap's been around forever... even in the days of the Ink Spots and the Mills Brothers.

— Quincy

"I used to walk in stores and yell 'Lay down.' You flinch an inch, AK spray down. But I was lucky 'cause I never caught the hard time. I was blessed with the skill to bust a dope rhyme. I'm not gonna lie to ya, 'cause I don't lie. I just kick thick game, some people say why. 'Cause I'm back on the block, got my life back." — Ice-T

(Lyrics from BOTB)

Rap has always touched me as being a very powerful form of narrative. In 1985 L.L. Cool J. said to me, "What do the singers and musicians think of us?" And that's the first time I realized that they think of themselves as a third entity. — Quincy

Ice-T

The times are always contained in the rhythm.

Big Daddy Kane

I walked by Big Daddy Kane when we were at the heat of our crunch in the album—and he's got his dictionary and his gangster hat on. There's a lot of drama with rappers and he's got his heaviest gangster look going on. He looks at me and calls me over to him, and says, "Let me hear you use 'sterile' in a sentence." And I know where he's coming from: He wants to rhyme 'sterile' with 'Ella Fitzgerald,' but he's not sure how the word is used. Rappers are thirsty, hungry minds trying to express themselves in a poetic and profound way. – Quincy

Hip hop in many ways is the same as bebop, because it was very renegade-type music. It came from a disenfranchised sub-culture that got thrown out of the way. They said, "We'll make up our own life. We'll have our own language." – Quincy

Kool Moe Dee

Flavor Flav

I think the most vital lyrics and statements are now being made by hip hop writers. And once they discover melody, they're going to have a field day. – Quincy

Rap is the most passionate music in America right now. The words slap people in the face with vivid, graphic reality. It's an urban network driven by a social, political motor. –Quincy

indication of Quincy's visionary attempts to show the continuity of the black musical tradition.

In "Secret Garden," the high tenors of Al B. Sure! and El DeBarge are shrewdly counterpointed by James Ingram's husky soul style and Barry White's deep bass, all running over a sexy R&B slow dance groove. First in solo passages and then in ensembles, the voices are arranged with the sensitivity Quincy once used on horns. "Wee B. Dooinit" pushes to an extreme the idea of voice as instrument. Under the name of Human Bean Band some of the greatest jazz singers in history—Sarah Vaughan and Ella Fitzgerald, Al Jarreau and Bobby McFerrin, youngbloods Take 6 and Garrett—all mesh in a rich tapestry of a cappella. Bruce Swedien even recorded the sounds Quincy made on his own body and ran them through an enhancer; beating his chest became a kick-drum sound, a scratched head a shaker. Quincy literally played himself to provide the backing track.

Back to back in the middle of the album are "The Places You Find Love" and "Jazz Corner of the World—Birdland," both ambitious and successful fusions of Quincy's favorite sounds. Garrett handles the swooping lead vocal with great passion while two separate choirs, one a gospel group conducted by Andrae Crouch, the other an all-star ensemble (Luther Vandross, Howard Hewitt, Dionne Warwick, Jennifer Holliday) back her up. A thicket of synthesizers plays against the soaring sound of choirs. Swahili lyrics written by Semenya turn a great pop song into an anthem of African-American and African cultural cooperation.

Quincy puts his belief in the bebop–hip hop connection on the line with "Jazz Corner of the World—Birdland." The voices and words of Kool Moe Dee and Big Daddy Kane provide a spunky, funky bebop history lesson in verse. The two rappers sketch out the importance of James Moody, Miles Davis, George Benson, Sarah Vaughan, Dizzy Gillespie, Ella Fitzgerald, and

YOU GOTTA WRITE YOUR OWN TICKET IN THIS LIFE BECAUSE IF YOU DON'T THEN SOMEBODY IS DEFINITELY GONNA WRITE A TICKET FOR YOU. AND YOU AIN'T GONNA RIDE FIRST CLASS. YOU'LL JUST FALL VICTIM TO WHATEVER THE STREET DICTATES TO YOU INSTEAD OF TRYING TO DICTATE SOMETHING TO THE STREET. —MELLE MEL

Weather Report founder Josef Zawinul, the rap rhymes intercut with brief solos by each of the legends named. The voice of Pee Wee Marquette, Birdland's immortal doorman, is heard as well. All this rapping leads to "Birdland" itself. Zawinul, who comes from the same jazz world as Quincy, wrote the song a decade ago, and it has since become a standard in the post-acoustic jazz repertoire. Quincy gives it new life by having Gillespie, Moody, George Benson, Vaughan, and Fitzgerald all take solos. The conjunction of these elements creates a fantastic, pungent effect, a time warp of tunes and tones. For fans of rap and aficionados of jazz, such a collaboration is totally unexpected. But throughout Quincy's life, he's never stopped with what is. He's always tried to find out what might be. Labels don't matter. For Quincy, good music is good music, and that's all he's ever made.

FAST FORWARD

It's winter in Southern California. Quincy Jones sits in front of a picture window overlooking the city of Los Angeles. The view is exhilarating. It's just finished raining, and for a few hours this smoggy metropolis has clean, clear air. You can see all the way downtown, but Quincy, curled up in a backless chair, his glasses perched on the tip of his nose, could not care less. Instead, he scans *Variety, Hollywood Reporter, Radio & Records,* and *Billboard*. Finally the phone rings. He scribbles down sothing then he smiles

The latest is coming in th work. He stud of a rookie pr phones. When he talks to friends and colleagues in the industry, Quincy isn't cocky or overconfident. He speculates on how competing projects may affect the record's sales. He gives and receives suggestions on the next single to release. He gossips, analyzes, schemes, and ▶ PG 178

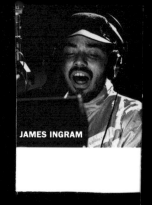

JAMES INGRAM

I WANTED TO MAKE AN ALBUM THAT INCORPORATED THE WHOLE FAMILY OF AMERICAN

BLACK MUSIC. FROM GOSPEL TO JAZZ, EVERYTHING THAT'S PART OF MY CULTURE. —QUINCY

AL B. SURE!

Big Daddy

Back up and give the brother room
To let poetry bloom to whom
It may concern or consume
As I reminisce before this
The bliss that exists
But now we brought about a twist
'Cause I remember reading of my people bleeding
Put through slavery and killed for bravery
We should have got our freedom much sooner
You never seen a black man on the "Honeymooners"
But now somehow we learn to earn
To grow, to show
The elevation that our people built is so
Jesse Jackson, Miss America, a black one
No more livin' for just a small fraction
I was once told by the Dude that knowledge is a food
To nourish
So to conclude
This from an Asiatic descendant, Big Daddy is shocked
Yo Q, we Back on the Block

Kane

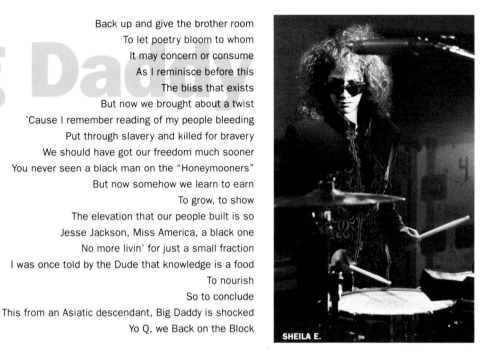
SHEILA E.

JAMES MOODY

SIEDAH GARRETT

MILES DAVIS

ANDRAE CROUCH

BIG DADDY KANE

HERBIE HANCOCK

ELLA FITZGERALD

CAIPHUS SEMENYA

GEORGE DUKE

the top, never fear 'cause I'm Back on the Block.

An everlasting omnipresence is my present
State of being seeing the unpleasant
Sight of righteous souls live like peasants
The mind stunts growth in adolescence
My insight enables me to enlight
The weakest of minds and put it in flight
As I transcend, ascend or descend
Recreate, re-incarnate and re-send
The powerful spirits of our ancestors
For those that don't know how God blessed us
Because man messed up
The media dressed up
Lies perpetrated as truths
And it left us confused
But I've seen it all before
From Babylon to the Third World War
I'm more than a man I'm more like an entity
Back on the Block this time my identity is
The Dude

Kool Moe Dee

QD III

CHILDREN'S CHOIR

DIZZY GILLESPIE

the block

B

ICE-T

I'm Back on the Block portraying the Dude ... So if you're ready to reach for

BRUCE SWEDIEN

BARRY WHITE

RAY CHARLES

Three people came up to me

to ask for an autograph.

One was a **grandmother,**

I guess she was in her late '50s,

and one was a **mother,**

probably late '20s,

and this **little girl**

that was about 11 or 12 years old.

And the little girl had

"We Are the World,"

and the mother had

"Thriller,"

and the grandmother had

"Sinatra at the Sands."

And it really touched me.

–Quincy

QUINCY C. 1955

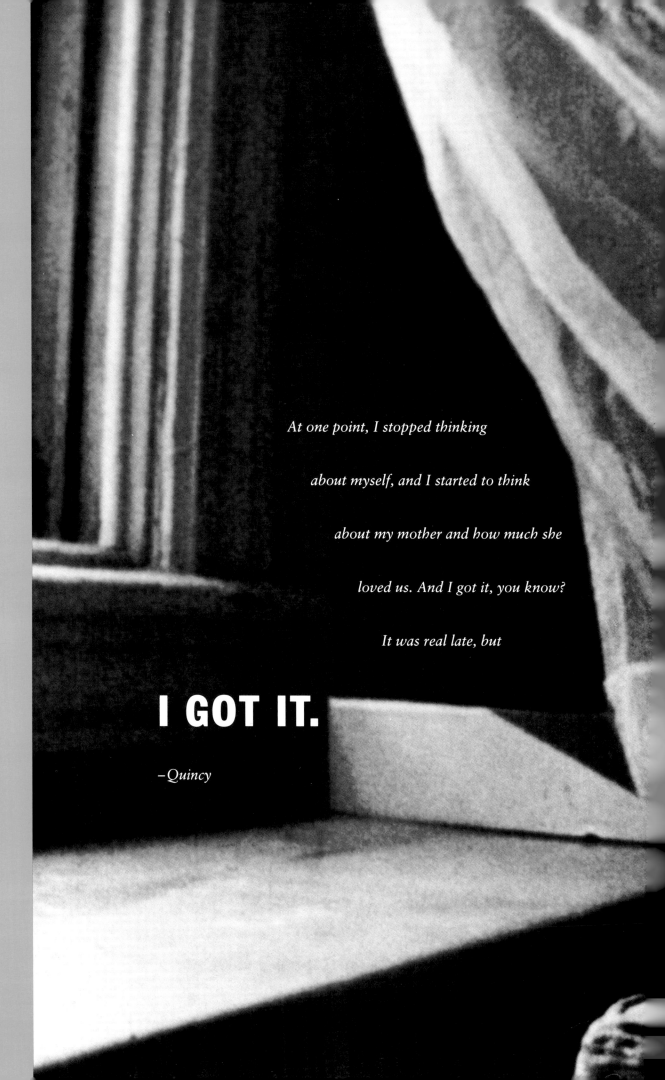

dreams—he's clearly still plugged in, still hungry.

The international awards and friendships, the multi-platinum albums, the films, the money, haven't dampened his desire to achieve. Maximum effort to achieve optimum results has been his unspoken credo. But the best description of why Quincy has persevered came in his reply to a question about what makes Michael Jackson great.

"When [Michael] commits to an idea, he goes all the way with it. He has the presence of mind to feel something, conceive it, and then bring it to life. It's a long way from idea to execution. Everybody wants to go to heaven and nobody wants to die. It's ass power, man. You have to be emotionally ready to put as much energy into it as it takes to make it right ... If you want to make something beautiful, you have to have the spiritual and physical knowledge to pace yourself, to make it through. Got to be ready to deal with infinite detail. Only the very best are."

If anyone in the thirties and forties had suggested to a black child growing up in Chicago and Seattle what the eighties and nineties would hold for black performers, he would have been regarded as clearly insane. But American children born since the civil rights era have grown up in a time of unprecedented racial integration in the entertainment media. By the end of the eighties, Eddie Murphy was America's biggest box-office draw, Oprah Winfrey and Arsenio Hall were the hottest talk-show hosts, Bill Cosby was America's favorite dad, and Michael Jordan was the most visible athlete. And the figure most associated with the richness, grandeur, and spirit of American music wasn't a European-American traditionalist like Aaron Copland, Lawrence Welk, or Leonard Bernstein, but an erstwhile trumpeter from Chicago's South Side whom his friends call Q.

At one point, I stopped thinking

about myself, and I started to think

about my mother and how much she

loved us. And I got it, you know?

It was real late, but

I GOT IT.

–Quincy

In the nineties, the interplay of music, image, and technology will surely take culture in creative and commercial directions we can only imagine now, and Quincy Jones will be right there leading the way. His experience in music and film make him incredibly well positioned not only to capitalize on the coming changes in how we communicate but to put his own very powerful stamp on the new decade. Despite his long history of achievement, Quincy shows no intention of retiring or even of slowing down. In fact, for Q, the best years may be yet to come.

It's a bitch to try to convert hate to love. And that's a tough trick. But if you do it, it's the only

salvation.

–Quincy

QUINCY'S KIDS, CLOCKWISE FROM BOTTOM: JOLIE, TROY BEYER (FAMILY FRIEND), QUINCY III, KIDADA, TINA, RACHEL, SUNNY (GRANDCHILD), RASHIDA, DONOVAN (GRANDCHILD)

LOVE, HE HAS TO BE SURROUNDED WITH IT, HE CANNOT SPEND ONE MOMENT WITHOUT IT, HE HAS TO BE SURROUNDED WITH HAPPINESS, WHEN THERE IS ONE BAD VIBRATION ANYWHERE, HE QUITS, HE LEAVES THE ROOM. —MICHEL LEGRAND

Maybe because he's

such a big figure in the

outside world,

We expect him to be this...

I'm very proud of what he does. And things he's made possible...for the world and for us.

this Quincy Jones of a father.

I don't know if that

even exists.

– Jolie Jones Levine

Abbreviations
AD = Adaptation
AR = Arranger
CD = Conductor
CP = Composer
DI = Director
EXPD = Executive Producer
KB = Keyboard
LD = Leader
MS = Musical Supervision
P = Piano
PD = Producer
T = Trumpet
VO = Vocal

Time Line

1933

Quincy Delight Jones, Jr., born in Chicago, March 14, to Quincy Delight and Sarah Jones.

1943

Family moves to Washington State, settling first in Bremerton, eventually moving to Seattle.

1947

Begins studying trumpet and other instruments. First public appearance, on French horn, at YMCA dance.

1948

Begins performing with **Bumps Blackwell** and other Seattle ensembles, jamming at local clubs with **Ray Charles** and others, and backing up local appearances by such singers as **Billie Holiday** and **Billy Eckstine.**

1950

Studies trumpet with **Clark Terry** in Seattle with the **Count Basie** group (Quincy begins lifelong friendship with Basie). First composition, "Nocturne in Blue," performed at high school recital.

1951

Accepts scholarship to Schillinger House in Boston (later renamed Berklee School of Music). Begins writing freelance arrangements for **Oscar Pettiford** and others in New York. Meets **Charlie Parker** and **Dizzy Gillespie.** Leaves Schillinger to join **Lionel Hampton**'s band as trumpeter and arranger. Spends three years with Hampton, including his first recording sessions and first tours of Europe.

Oscar Pettiford: *The New Oscar Pettiford Sextet* (Debut DLP-8)
AR/CP

Various arrangements, compositions, and instrumental work for **Lionel Hampton** (including "Kingfish," his first recorded composition).

1952

Arrangements and compositions for **Al Grey.**

1953

Leaves **Lionel Hampton** and begins busy freelance career in New York as arranger, composer, conductor, and trumpeter. Daughter, **Jolie,** born to **Quincy** and **Jeri Caldwell.**

Quincy Jones's Swedish American All-Stars (Prestige LP-172)
CP/AR/CD

Art Farmer Septet Plays Arrangements of Gigi Gryce & Quincy Jones (Prestige P-7031)
CP/AR/P

Art Farmer: *Work of Art* (Prestige LP-162)
CP/AR/P

Clifford Brown: *New Star on the Horizon* (Blue Note BLP-5032)
CP/AR

Clifford Brown/Art Farmer: *Stockholm Sweetnin'* (Metronome MEP18 & 19)
CP/AR/DI

Miscellaneous:
Various arrangements, compositions, production, and instrumental work for **Gigi Gryce, Russell Jacquet, James Moody, George Wallington, Clifford Solomon.**

1954

James Moody's Moods (Prestige LP-192)
CP/AR

Oscar Pettiford (Bethlehem BCP-1003)
CP/AR

Introducing Joe Gordon (EmArcy MG-26046)
CP/AR

Go! Go! Go!: The Treniers on TV (Epic 9127)
AR/LD

Helen Merrill (EmArcy MG-36006)
AR

Harry Lookofsky: *Miracle in Strings* (Epic EG-7081)
CP/AR

Miscellaneous:
Various arrangements, compositions, and production for **Willie Mays, Hank D'Amico, George Wallington, Dizzy Gillespie, Art Mardigan, Ray Anthony, Ray Wheaton, Four Joes, Paul Quinichette, King Pleasure, Sam Most, the Sandmen, Oscar Pettiford, Aaron Sachs, James Moody, Dinah Washington.**

1955

Quincy Jones: *The Giants of Jazz* (Columbia CL-1970)
CP/AR/CD/LD

Quincy Jones: *Lullaby of Birdland* (RCA Victor LPM-1146)
CD/AR

Clark Terry (EmArcy MG-36007)
CP/AR

Dinah Washington: *For Those in Love* (Mercury MG-36011)
AR/CD

Meet Betty Carter & Ray Bryant (Epic LN-3202)
AR/LD

Julian "Cannonball" Adderley (EmArcy MG-36043)
CP/AR/DI

Introducing Jimmy Cleveland & His All Stars (EmArcy MG-36066)
CP/AR/DI

The Finest of Oscar Pettiford (Bethlehem BCP-6007)
CP/AR

Sonny Stitt Plays Arrangements from the Pen of Quincy Jones (Roost LP-2204)
CP/AR/CD

James Moody: *Wail Moody, Wail* (Prestige LP-7036)
CP/AR

Miscellaneous:
Various arrangements, compositions, and production for **The Four Joes, Lurlean Hunter, Brook Benton, Chuck Willis, Herbie Mann, the Sandmen, Leo Anthony, Delores Hawkins, the Honeytones, Bill Davis, Big Maybelle, Evelyn Knight, Sam Taylor, Eddie "Tex" Curtis, George Brunis, Tommy Coles, Lou Stein, Carmen Taylor, Betty Cox, Gigi Gryce, Vi Velasco, Ethel Smith, Jon Hendricks, Helene Dixon, Don Elliott.**

1956

Becomes musical director, arranger, and trumpeter for **Dizzy Gillespie** Orchestra's State Department tour of Europe, the Middle East, and South America.

Quincy Jones: *This Is How I Feel About Jazz* (ABC Paramount ABC-149)
CP/AR/LD

Gene Krupa: *Drummer Man* (Verve MGV-2008)
AR

Dizzy Gillespie: *World Statesman* (Norgran MG N-1084)
CP/AR/T

Dizzy Gillespie: *Dizzy in Greece* (Verve MGV-8017)
CP/AR/T

The Great Ray Charles
(Atlantic SD-1259)
CP/AR

Dinah Washington: *The Swingin' Miss D*
(EmArcy MG-36104)
CP/AR/LD

Various arrangements, compositions, instrumental work, and production for **Lily Ann Carol, the Cardinals, the Crew Cuts, Thad Jones, Ralph Marterie, Louis Jordan, Harry Lookofsky, Diahann Carroll.**

1957
Relocates to Paris for 18 months where he conducts and arranges numerous recording sessions and concert tours and works as A&R man for Barclay Records. Studies with **Nadia Boulanger**. Marries **Jeri Caldwell**.

Quincy Jones: *Go West, Man*
(ABC-Paramount ABC-186)
PD

Quincy Jones: *Un Soir a Paris (A Nite in Paris)* (Barclay 80.101)
AR/CP

Milt Jackson: *Plenty, Plenty Soul* (Atlantic 1269)
CP/AR

Billy Taylor: *My Fair Lady Loves Jazz*
(ABC Paramount ABC-177)
AR/CD

Jackie & Roy: *Bits and Pieces*
(ABC Paramount ABC-163)
AR

Art Farmer: *Last Night When We Were Young*
(ABC Paramount ABC-200)
AR/CD

Eddie Barclay: *Et Voila*
(Barclay 82.138)
AR

Miscellaneous:
Various arrangements, compositions, and production for **Bob Martin, Louis Jordan, the Clovers, Willis Jackson, June Richmond, LaVern Baker, Joe Newman, Billy Eckstine.**

1958
Harry Arnold + Big Band + Quincy Jones = Jazz!
(Metronome MLP-15010)
CP/AR/CD

Sarah Vaughan: *Vaughan and Violins*
(Mercury MG-20370)
CP/AR/CD

Count Basie: *Basie: One More Time*
(Roulette SR-52024)
CP/AR

Various arrangements and compositions for **Eddie Barclay, Henri Salvador, the Blue Stars.**

1959
Signs on as musical director of *Free and Easy*, a **Harold Arlen** blues opera set to tour Europe, and organizes all-star big band for the show. When the show falls through, keeps the band together for extensive touring in Europe throughout 1960, including several dates accompanying **Nat Cole** and others. Financial troubles with tour force him to sell his publishing catalogue.

Quincy Jones: *The Birth of a Band* (Mercury MG-20444)
CP/AR/LD

Quincy Jones: *The Birth of a Band, Vol. 2* (Mercury 195J-30)
CP/AR/LD

The Great Wide World of Quincy Jones
(Mercury SR-60221)
CD/LD
Grammy nomination: Best Jazz Performance, Large Group

The Ballad Artistry of Milt Jackson (Atlantic SD-1342)
P/AR/CD

Count Basie, Billy Eckstine: *Basie-Eckstine, Inc.* (Roulette SR-52050)
AR

The Genius of Ray Charles (Atlantic 1312)
AR
Grammy nomination: Best Arrangement, "Let the Good Times Roll"

Count Basie: *String Along with Basie* (Roulette R-52051)
CP/AR

Miscellaneous:
Various arrangements, compositions, and/or conducting for **Helen Merrill, June Eckstine, Illinois Jacquet, Sascha Burland.**

1960
Quincy Jones: *I Dig Dancers*
(Mercury SR-60612)
CP/AR/CD
Grammy nomination: Best Performance by an Orchestra for Dancing

Andy Williams: *Under Paris Skies* (Cadence CLP-3047)
AR/CD

Ray Charles: *Genius + Soul = Jazz* (Impulse AS-2)
AR

Double Six of Paris: *The Double Six Meet Quincy Jones* (French Columbia FPX 188 SEG-8088)
CD/CP/AR

1961
Takes A&R job with Mercury Records in New York, rising, in 1964, to vice president of Mercury. Begins touring as musical director for various singers. Earns first Grammy nominations (for his own *The Great Wide World of Quincy Jones* LP and for arrangement of "Let the Good Times Roll" for **Ray Charles**). Scores his first film, *The Boy in the Tree*.

Quincy Jones: *Around the World* (Mercury PPS-6014)
AR/CP/CD

The Great Wide World of Quincy Jones – Live!
(Mercury 195J-32)
AR/CD

Quincy Jones: *Newport '61*
(Mercury SR-60653)
CP/AR/CD

Quincy Jones: *The Quintessence* (Impulse A-11)
CP/AR/CD
Grammy nomination: Best Original Jazz Composition, *Quintessence*; Best Instrumental Arrangement, *Quintessence*

Quincy Jones: *The Boy in the Tree* (soundtrack)
(Mercury-Sweden EP-60338)
AR/CP/CD

Peggy Lee: *If You Go*
(Capitol T-1630)
AR/CD

Peggy Lee: *Blues Cross Country* (Capitol ST-1671)
CP/AR/CD

Dinah Washington: *Tears and Laughter* (Mercury SR-60661)
DI/CD/LD

Brook Benton: *There Goes That Song Again*
(Mercury MG-20673)
AR

Billy Eckstine & Quincy Jones at Basin Street East
(Mercury SR-60674)
AR/CD

Joe Newman Quintet at Count Basie's (Mercury SR-60696)
PD

Dinah Washington: *I Wanna Be Loved* (Mercury MG-20729)
CP/AR/CD

1962
Quincy Jones: *Big Band Bossa Nova* (Mercury MG-20751)
LD/AR/CP/PD
Grammy nomination: Best Performance by an Orchestra for Dancing

Dizzy Gillespie: *New Wave* (Philips PHM-200-070)
PD

Dizzy Gillespie: *Dizzy on the French Riviera*
(Philips PHM 200-048)
PD

Sarah Vaughan: *You're Mine You* (Roulette R-52082)
AR/CD

Harry Lookofsky: *The Hash Brown Sounds* (Philips PHM 200-018)
PD

Miscellaneous: Produced albums for **Billy Eckstine** and **Damita Jo, the Three Sounds, Bobby Scott.**

1963

Wins first Grammy Award (for arrangement of "I Can't Stop Loving You" for **Count Basie Orchestra**). Discovers **Lesley Gore** and produces his first number-one single, Gore's "It's My Party." Scores his first Hollywood film, *The Pawnbroker.*

Quincy Jones: *Quincy Jones Plays the Hip Hits* (Mercury SR-60799)
CD/AR
Grammy nomination: Best Instrumental Jazz Performance, Large Group; Best Performance by an Orchestra for Dancing

The Golden Hits of Billy Eckstine (Mercury SR-60796)
PD

Terry Gibbs Plays Jewish Melodies in Jazztime (Mercury MG-20812)
PD

Count Basie: *This Time by Basie* (Reprise R-6070)
AR/CD
Grammy Award: Best Instrumental Arrangement, "I Can't Stop Loving You"

Count Basie: *Li'l Ol' Groovemaker...Basie!* (Verve V6-8549)
CP/AR/CD

Ella Fitzgerald/Count Basie: *Ella and Basie* (Verve MGV-4061)
AR/CD

Three Sounds: *Some Like It Modern* (Mercury SR-60839)
DI

Sarah Vaughan: *Sassy Swings the Tivoli* (Mercury MG-20831)
DI

Sarah Vaughan: *Vaughn with Voices* (Mercury MG-20882)
PD

Shirley Horn with Horns (Mercury MG-20835)
PD/CD/AR/LD

Lesley Gore: *I'll Cry if I Want To* (Mercury MG-20805)
PD/DI

1964

Quincy Jones Explores the Music of Henry Mancini (Mercury MG-20863)
AR/CD/LD
Grammy nomination: Best Instrumental Jazz Performance, Large Group or Soloist with Large Group

Quincy Jones: *Golden Boy* (Mercury MG-20938)
CP/AR/CD/LD
Grammy nominations: Best Original Jazz Composition, "The Witching Hour"; Best Instrumental Performance, Non-Jazz, "Golden Boy" (String Version); Best Instrumental Arrangement, "Golden Boy" (String Version)

Quincy Jones: *We Had a Ball* (Mercury MG-21022)
AR/CD

Quincy Jones: *The Pawnbroker* (soundtrack) (Mercury 1011)
PD/CP/AR/CD

Billy Eckstine: *The Modern Sound of Mr. B.* (Mercury SR-60916)
PD

Frank Sinatra/Count Basie: *It Might As Well Be Swing* (Reprise FS-1012)
AR/CD

Sarah Vaughan: *VIVA! Vaughan* (Mercury MG-20941)
PD

Sammy Davis/Count Basie: *Our Shining Hour* (Verve V6-8605)
AR/CD

Lesley Gore: *Boys, Boys, Boys* (Mercury MG-20901)
PD

Lesley Gore: *Girl Talk* (Mercury MG-20943)
PD

Produced albums for **Julius Watkins, Robert Farnon, Damita Jo, David Carroll, Timi Yuro, the Three Sounds.**

1965

Leaves Mercury Records and relocates to Southern California to begin full-time work as film composer.

Quincy Jones: *Quincy Plays for Pussycats* (Mercury MG-21050)
AR/CD

Quincy Jones: *Quincy's Got a Brand-New Bag* (Mercury MG-21063)
PD/AR/CD

Quincy Jones: *Mirage* (soundtrack) (Mercury MG-21025)
CP/AR/CD

Sarah Vaughan Sings the Mancini Songbook (Mercury MG-21009)
PD

Lesley Gore: *My Town, My Guy & Me* (Mercury MG-21042)
PD

1966

Daughter, **Tina**, born. **Jeri Jones** and **Quincy** divorce.
Quincy Jones: *Walk, Don't Run* (soundtrack) (Mainstream S-6080)
CP/CD

Quincy Jones: *The Slender Thread* (soundtrack) (Mercury MG-21070)
CP/CD

Frank Sinatra/Count Basie: *Sinatra at the Sands* (Reprise 1019)
AR/CD

1967

Marries **Ulla Anderson**. Scores the pilot and eight episodes of *Ironside.*

Quincy Jones: *The Deadly Affair* (soundtrack) (Verve V6-8679-ST)
CP/CD

Quincy Jones: *Enter Laughing* (soundtrack) (Liberty LOM-16004)
CP/CD

Quincy Jones: *In the Heat of the Night* (soundtrack) (United Artists UAL-4160)
CP/CD
Grammy nomination: Best Original Score Written for Motion Picture or Television Show

Quincy Jones: *In Cold Blood* (soundtrack) (Colgems COM-107)
CP/CD
Academy Award nomination: Best Original Score

Other films: *Banning* (Academy Award nomination: Best Song, "The Eyes of Love"–with Bob Russell)

1968

Son, **Quincy Delight Jones III**, born.

Quincy Jones: *For Love of Ivy* (soundtrack) (ABC ABCS-OC-7)
CP/CD
Academy Award nomination: Best Song, "For Love of Ivy"—with Bob Russell

Other films: *Jigsaw, A Dandy in Aspic, The Hell with Heroes, The Split, Up Your Teddy Bear, Jocelyn.*

1969

Begins recording for A & M Records. *Walking in Space* first of ten albums for the label.

Quincy Jones: *Walking in Space* (A & M SP-3023)
AR/CD
Grammy Award: Best Instrumental Jazz Performance, Large Group or Soloist with Large Group, *Walking in Space*; Grammy nomination: Best Instrumental Arrangement, *Walking in Space*

Quincy Jones: *Mackenna's Gold* (soundtrack) (RCA Victor LSP-4096)
PD/CP/CD/AR
Grammy nomination: Best Instrumental Theme, *Mackenna's Gold* (Main Title)

Quincy Jones: *The Italian Job* (soundtrack) (Paramount PAS-5007)
CP/CD

Quincy Jones: *The Lost Man* (soundtrack) (Uni 73060)
PD/CP
Grammy nomination: Best Original Score Written for Motion Picture or Television Show

Quincy Jones: *Bob & Carol & Ted & Alice* (soundtrack) (Bell 1200)
PD/CD/AR/CP

Quincy Jones: *John and Mary* (soundtrack) (A & M SP-4230)
PD/CP/CD

1970
Scores *The Bill Cosby Show*, totaling 56 episodes, including theme, "Hicky Burr: The Ballad of Chet Kincaid."

Quincy Jones: *Gula Matari* (A & M SP-3030)
CP/AR/CD
Grammy nominations: Best Jazz Performance, Large Group or Soloist with Large Group, **Gula Matari**; Best Instrumental Arrangement, **Gula Matari**; Best Instrumental Composition, **Gula Matari**

Quincy Jones: *Cactus Flower* (soundtrack) (Bell 1201)
PD/CD/AR/CP

Quincy Jones: *They Call Me Mister Tibbs* (soundtrack) (United Artists UAS-5214)
PD/CP/CD
Grammy nomination: Best Contemporary Instrumental Performance, *Soul Flower*

Ringo Starr: *Sentimental Journey* (Apple SW-3365)
AR

Other films: *The Last of the Mobile Hotshots, The Out-of-Towners, Sheila.*

1971
Quincy Jones: *Smackwater Jack* (A & M SP-3037)
PD/CP/AR/CD/VO
Grammy Award: Best Pop Instrumental Performance

Quincy Jones: *Dollars* (soundtrack) (Reprise MS-2051)
PD/CP/AR/CD
Grammy nominations: Best Instrumental Arrangement, "Money Runner"; Best Pop Instrumental by Arranger, Composer, and Orchestra, "Money Runner"; Best Original Score Written for Motion Picture

J. J. Johnson: *Man and Boy* (soundtrack) (Sussex SXSB-7011)
PD

1972
Helps organize Black EXPO in Chicago with the **Rev. Jesse Jackson** to raise awareness and money for Operation PUSH (People United to Save Humanity). Scores the *Bill Cosby* variety series, totaling 27 episodes. Writes theme for NBC *Mystery* series.

Quincy Jones: *You've Got It Bad Girl* (A & M SP-3041)
PD/CP/AR/CD/VO
Grammy Award: Best Instrumental Arrangement, "Summer in the City"; Grammy nomination: Best Pop Instrumental Performance

Quincy Jones: *The Hot Rock* (soundtrack) (Prophesy SD-6055)
PD/CP/AR/CD

Aretha Franklin: *Hey Now Hey (The Other Side of the Sky)* (Atlantic SD-7265)
PD/AR/CD

Donny Hathaway: *Come Back Charleston Blue* (soundtrack) (Atco SD-7010)
CP/MS

Other films: *Yao of the Jungle, The New Centurions.*

1973
Spearheads formation of IBAM (Institute for Black American Music) and Operation Breadbasket with the **Rev. Jesse Jackson.** Organizes television salute to **Duke Ellington,** *...We Love You Madly.* Writes *Sanford and Son* theme.

1974
Ulla Jones and **Quincy** divorce. Marries **Peggy Lipton.** Suffers two brain aneurysms. Daughter, **Kidada,** born.

Quincy Jones: *Body Heat* (A & M SP-3617)
PD/CP/AR/CD/VO
Grammy nomination: Best Pop Vocal Performance, Duo or Group; Best Pop Instrumental Performance, "Body Heat"

1975
Quincy Jones: *Mellow Madness* (A & M SP-4526)
PD/CP/AR/KB/T/VO/CD

1976
Daughter, **Rashida,** born.

Quincy Jones: *I Heard That!!* (A & M SP-3705)
PD/CP/CD/AR/KB/VO/T
Grammy nomination: Best Instrumental Composition, "Midnight Soul Patrol"—with **Louis Johnson, Johnny Mandel**

Brothers Johnson: *Look Out for #1* (A & M SP-4567)
PD/AR/CP

Lesley Gore: *Love Me By Name* (A & M SP-4564)
PD/AR/CP/CD/KB/VO

1977
Scores *Roots,* the most-watched series in television history.

Quincy Jones: *Roots* (TV soundtrack) (A & M SP-4626)
PD/CP/AR/CD
Grammy nominations: Best Arrangement for Voices, "Oh Lord, Come By Here"—with **James Cleveland, Johnny Mandel;** Best Inspiration Performance, "Oh, Lord, Come By Here"—with **James Cleveland, Johnny Mandel;** Best Instrumental Composition, "Roots Medley"—with **Gerald Fried**

Brothers Johnson: *Right on Time* (A & M SP-4644)
PD/AR/CP

1978
Scores *The Wiz,* his first working relationship with **Michael Jackson.**

Quincy Jones: *Sounds...And Stuff Like That* (A & M SP-4685)
PD/AR/CP
Grammy nomination: Best Arrangement for Voices, "Stuff Like That"—with **Nick Ashford, Valerie Simpson**

Quincy Jones: *The Wiz* (soundtrack) (MCA MCA 2-14000)
PD/CD/CP/AR/AD/MS/KB
Grammy Award: Best Instrumental Arrangement, "Main Title (Overture Part One)"—with **Robert Freedman**; Grammy nomination: Best Instrumental Composition, "End of the Yellow Brick Road"—with **Nick Ashford, Valerie Simpson.** Academy Award Nomination: Best Score Adaptation

Brothers Johnson: *Blam!* (A & M SP-4685)
PD/AR/CP
Grammy nomination: Best Producer, 1978

1979
Michael Jackson: *Off the Wall* (Epic FE-35745)
PD/AR
Grammy nomination: Best Disco Recording, "Don't Stop Till You Get Enough"—with **Michael Jackson**

Rufus & Chaka Khan: *Masterjam* (MCA MCA-5103)
PD/CP
Grammy nomination: Best Producer, 1979

1980
Forms Qwest Records and Qwest Music Group.

George Benson: *Give Me the Night* (Qwest HS-3453)
PD/AR
Grammy Award: Best Instrumental Arrangement, "Dinorah, Dinorah"—with **Jerry Hey**

Brothers Johnson: *Light Up the Night* (A & M SP-3716)
PD/AR/VO
Grammy nomination: Best Producer, 1980

1981
Quincy Jones: *The Dude* (A & M SP-3721)
PD/CP/AR/VO
Grammy Awards: Best R&B Performance by Duo or Group with Vocal, "The Dude"; Best Arrangement on an Instrumental Recording, "Velas"—with **Johnny Mandel**; Best Instrumental Arrangement Accompanying Vocal, "Ai No Corrida"—with **Jerry Hey**; Grammy nominations: Album of the Year; Best Pop Instrumental Performance, "Velas"

Quincy Jones: *Live at the Budokan* (A & M AMP-28045) 1981
CD/PD/CP/AR/KB

Patti Austin: *Every Home Should Have One* (Qwest QWS-3591)
PD/AR

Ernie Watts: *Chariots of Fire* (Qwest QWS-3637)
PD/CP/AR

Lena Horne: *The Lady and Her Music* (Qwest 2QW-3597)
PD
Grammy Awards: Best Cast Show Album; Producer of the Year, 1981

1982
Michael Jackson: *Thriller* (Epic QE-38112)
PD/AR/CP
Grammy Awards: Album of the Year—with **Michael Jackson**; Record of the Year, *Beat It*—with **Michael Jackson**; Grammy nomination: Best R&B Instrumental Performance, "Billie Jean" (Instrumental Version)—with **Jerry Hey**

Michael Jackson: *E.T., the Extraterrestrial* (MCA MCA-70000)
PD
Grammy Award: Best Recording for Children

Donna Summer: *Donna Summer* (Geffen GHS-2005)
PD/AR/CP/VO
Grammy Award: Producer of the Year, 1982

1983
James Ingram: *It's Your Night* (Qwest 1-23970)
PD/AR/CP/P/VO
Grammy nomination: Best R&B Song, "Yah Mo Be There"—with **James Ingram, Michael McDonald, Rod Temperton**; Grammy Award: Producer of the Year, 1983—with **Michael Jackson**

1984
Patti Austin (Qwest 1-23974)
PD

Frank Sinatra: *L.A. Is My Lady* (Qwest 25145-1)
PD/CP/AR/CD

Various Artists: *The Official Music of the XXIIIrd Olympiad L.A. 1984* (Columbia BJS-39322)
PD/CP/AR
Grammy Award: Best Arrangement of an Instrumental, "Grace (Gymnastics Theme)"—with **Jerry Lubbock**

1985
Co-produces *The Color Purple*, hiring **Steven Spielberg** as director and discovering **Oprah Winfrey.**

Quincy Jones: *The Color Purple* (soundtrack) (Qwest 25389-1)
PD/CP/AR/CD

Various Artists: "We Are the World" (single) (Columbia US2-05179)
PD/CD
Grammy Awards: Record of the Year; Best Pop Performance by a Duo or Group with Vocal; Best Music Video, Short Form—with **Tom Trbovich**; Grammy nomination: Album of the Year: *We Are the World/The Album*

Hubert Laws–Quincy Jones–Chick Corea (CBS Masterworks M-39858)
CD

1986
James Ingram: *Never Felt So Good* (Qwest 1-25424)
EXPD

1987
Michael Jackson: *Bad* (Epic OE-40600)
PD/AR
Grammy nominations: Album of the Year; Record of the Year, "Man in the Mirror"—with **Michael Jackson**; Producer of the Year—with **Michael Jackson**

1988
Grammy Award: Special Trustees Award

1989
Quincy Jones: *Back on the Block* (Qwest 26020-1)
PD/CP/AR/VO/CD

1990
Peggy Lipton-Jones and **Quincy** divorce. Forms the **Quincy Jones Entertainment Company**, a multimedia entertainment company. QJEC produces *The Fresh Prince of Bel Air* and *The Jesse Jackson Show* for the 1990-91 television season. Forms **Quincy Jones Broadcasting** to acquire television and radio properties.

Note: page numbers in *italics* refer to photographs.

Special thanks to Time Inc. Magazines Picture Collection.

**Based on the Warner Bros.
Motion Picture
LISTEN UP
The Lives of Quincy Jones**

Warner Bros. Presents
A Courtney Sale Ross Production
LISTEN UP
The Lives of Quincy Jones
Edited by Milton Moses
Ginsberg, Pierre Khan,
Andrew Morreale, Laurie
Sullivan, Paul Zehrer
Music by Quincy Jones
Music Supervisor
Arthur Baker
Director of Photography
Stephen Kazmierski
Line Producer
Melissa Powell
Produced by
Courtney Sale Ross
Directed by
Ellen Weissbrod